Building Life Muscles

Sta [illegible] **na**

"Trus [illegible] verse has your back"

MindBody Publishing

Published in the UK by MindBody Publishing

www.MindBodyPublishing.net

Also by the Authors

Books

The Calming Book of Healing Hugs

Power Up for the Year by Karen Burke

Music

Last Train to Calmsville by Devon Burke (Magus & Magus)

http://phore.st/52lj8

Products

MindBody Range
(including the new Healing Hug room mists)

Carib range

http://phore.st/r3Gyf

Acknowledgements
Thank you to the Universe.

Thank you to our children, who as young adults, still teach us the most, even though we may not admit it to them.

Thank you to all our family and friends for your continual love and support.

Thank you to all our teams and the people we have come across in our pathways and to all the people we have yet to meet.

To all the lessons learned and all the lessons we still need to learn.

Dedicated to those who try to be the best version of themselves.

'Today is the outcome of yesterday,
Tomorrow is the outcome of Today.
You Choose.'

Karen Burke

CONTENTS

Rainbows Within The Rain

Rainbows within the rain
Are like tiny buds of hope
When all seems dark and cloudy
Look up… 'See… we CAN cope'

They say 'Rome was not built in a day'
And we say 'but when is it going to change?'
Shhh! Nature is saying…
Can't you see what I'm trying to arrange

Do I ask you to replant the daffodil bulbs?
Do I say go trim the trees that flower?
Yet every spring they pop up almost unannounced
But do they appear out of nowhere?

No, for when the ground is frosted over
And the rain is slowly falling
All the preparation is taking place unseen
Meanwhile the buds are still growing

Does it feel like your world has just stopped?
Or that you've stepped in sinking sand?
'Oh…when is it going to happen to me?
When am I going to step on dry land?'
Hey! Never, ever, ever, give up hope
Never, ever think it only happens to some
Learn or unlearn, make choices, take action
Always know a change is going to come

But yes, Life may totally flip the script
And it may not happen in your timing or your way

But what has your name on it, is yours
So maybe, Life is just waiting for us to say

'Okay, okay, I get it' or 'okay I'll let it go'

For if spring doesn't lead to summer, autumn and winter
How will spring ever come around again?

Our life here is just a snippet of the universe
Know that seeds take time to grow
Busy, active, sitting still, waiting... keep it relative
And allow nature to unfold

In the meantime... Do, Be, Feel, Enjoy
Be the Greatest You, you can be
And experience life...

One day at a time... one step at a time

Deep breath... release... then look up...

Can you NOW see the beautiful rainbow within the rain?
Like tiny buds of hope
When all seems dark and cloudy

'See... I know you CAN cope.'

-Karen Burke 2007

Letter to the reader

We have all had times in life when we feel so ecstatic that we can hardly contain ourselves, and other times when we have been so overwhelmed that we don't know what to do, where to go or who to go to.

This book will help you to build stronger life muscles so you not only survive in the harsh times, but also flourish in both mind and body in the good times.

As individuals, we may reach out to something or someone to help hold us together in times of desperation. We look to them to say the words to help us. There is no shame in reaching out for help, however there will come a time when we have to reach into ourselves when we are alone, sitting with uncomfortable feelings in the quiet of the day and/or night.

We call this going through the 'eye of the needle': challenging times where the only way out is through. It is here when we need to be kind to ourselves as we go within to heal, to soothe our fears, aches and pains, and to make the resolve that we are going to get through this.

However, going through this eye should not be at the cost of your core being, the part of you that may need a healing hug during hard times. It is here where we would like you to be kind to yourself and create a safe space to BE for a while. It can be hard work, but we promise you that once you've built your life muscles, you can use them time and time again. Life will always throw us curveballs, but you will have better tools to manage it all.

So we have a promise that we'd like you to make to yourself as you go through this book, and as you go through your daily journey building those life muscles.

The Promise to Myself

I will continue to:

- ☐ Treat myself as I would treat others, so I will be kind to myself
- ☐ Take off the 'big boots' I kick myself with and kindly pat myself on the back more often
- ☐ Respect myself
- ☐ Not play the blame game but accept responsibility for my actions
- ☐ Not be judgmental with myself: I am at where I'm at right now
- ☐ Not compare myself with others but to celebrate me
- ☐ Not take everything personally or make too many assumptions
- ☐ Not be afraid to smile when all around me is gloomy
- ☐ Release resentment and regret; no shoulda, woulda, coulda
- ☐ Accept that the only person I can choose to change is myself
- ☐ Accept that learning and growth takes time
- ☐ Accept I cannot rush out of dark places if I need to sit there
- ☐ Allow my light to glow
- ☐ Be honest with myself.

Know that you have this promise, and can come to this safe and grounding space, at any time when life seems too harsh or you need a pick me up. You do not have to be 'on the go' all the time striving for growth. It is more important to be at peace with where you are while consciously choosing to change, if and when you feel you need to 'do better, be better'.

Safe space to just…BE

Taking a breather

When you need to feel comfortable and at peace with yourself, no matter if you are feeling weak or strong, build in 16 minutes a day[a] for 'daydreaming' and 'stillness', which can help to recalibrate and reorganise thoughts; giving the mind, body, soul and spirit the rest it craves before moving forward again.

[a]Dr Caroline Leaf talks about reshaping the brain by being still for 16mins – listen to one of her podcasts for a deep dive but we explain further in the Reset section.

Take a breather…

go into your safe space

1) Sit comfortably or lay down, with your head supported
2) Allow your mind to be still or drift into some pleasant thought or place
3) Think of encouraging words you would like to say to yourself (if unsure, think of what you would say to someone else)

Such as:

"I'm in a safe place"

"It's going to be okay"
"I've made it"
"I've survived"
"It will be even better going forward"
"Be calm"
"It is all happening perfectly right now"
"Be easy with yourself"

4) Feel the words emanating around your body as you take a long deep breath in and out
5) Slowly breathe in for the count of six, taking air into your lungs and breath out for the count of six
6) Breathe in these positive thoughts and breathe out only negative thoughts
7) Allow your body to let go of any tension and frustration as you sink into the chair, couch or bed
8) Tell yourself your head is clearing and you have feelings of calm, tranquillity and peace
9) Stay there for as long as you can or need before coming back consciously into your space.

You can come back here at any time and repeat the whole process. The more you repeat it the more effortless it becomes until it automatically becomes a part of your daily life as one of your tools to cope, thus helping you on the road to building life muscles.

Introduction

In the same way that the physical muscles support our whole body system, which is essential for a good healthy body, our internal life muscles support us mentally, emotionally and spiritually, developing an inner strength we can build and draw upon throughout life.

This book will show you how to build life muscles to enhance your personal growth, to improve resilience and build emotional stamina while staying rooted, grounded and balanced; that is, if you choose to change.

Throughout every microsecond of our day, we make mini choices on how we want our life to go. The Universe will contrive to make it happen. Every time we choose to change, to 'do better or be better', we build a life muscle.

You may already have been through many challenging storms in life, be dealing with life changing events right now, or just starting out in life. Whatever stage of life's journey you are at, the Building Life Muscles program, plus any future materials and workshops, can act as a guide to enable you to flourish. Working on yourself in this way can in turn help you to help others along their journey.

Both myself and Devon are coming from years of helping people to build life muscles, through building our own therapy businesses, from working in the corporate sector, to starting a social enterprise and building teams along the way. Many people have asked us over the years, 'How do you do it?' or 'How do you keep your energy up?' We respond that we try to look after our mind, body, soul and spirit, learning from our mistakes and building life muscles as we go along. We hope there will be many more answers for you in this book.

We have been in some of the spaces you may be in right now, so within the book we will share some of our stories and life experiences. We hope it will help you to recognise that we are all human and we are all learning how to do this thing called 'life'. We are sharing in this human experience and hopefully providing practical demonstrations of building a positive mindset from our own adversity.

We will take you on a journey to becoming more aware of:

- Where you are at in life
- What your natural thought processes are
- What your fall back and reset position is: how you deal with daily situations
- Your emotional and practical experiences, using quick daily tools and techniques to deal with emotions such as loss, disappointment and anger, while also staying happy and content
- Using your life muscles with your partner, your family, your work, in business and dealing with money, all big areas that can affect us in different seasons of life.

We will also share what we call Teachment© which is a word our family uses to describe the 'ancient knowing and wisdom, passed down through the generations to build emotional, mental and spiritual tools to survive, live and thrive'.

We encourage you to go through the exercises in this book. Either write in the book or have your own notepad or journal to log thoughts, feelings, emotions, as well as your own memories and stories along the way. This can help you to:

- Look back and realise just how far you have come
- Rediscover other parts of yourself
- Realise just how much strength you already have.

The fact that you have bought this book is a great first step, indicating that you are ready to increase your self-awareness and build your own life muscles. While you are reading this book, stay rooted and balanced, trusting that the Universe has your Back and knowing that you have more power than you ever imagined to do this thing called LIFE.

PART ONE
Building Life Muscles

Chapter 1

Why life muscles are needed

Physically, building muscles can help us to lose weight as muscle tissue burns more calories per day than fat tissue, even when at rest. Building muscle is healthy for your heart. That's because it can perform better with less oxygen, meaning the heart doesn't have to pump too hard when you are active.

Physical fitness

Building physical muscles can also help us to:

- Improve balance, sleep and mental health
- Reduce likelihood of falls
- Improve and help with blood sugar control
- Enhance power when moving, walking and running
- Cushion bones to prevent jarring bones
- Impact our energy and mobility
- Build strength and stamina
- Help control body fat and get rid of excess weight
- Build self-confidence, thus changing our emotional state and ability to attract.

Once we start a keep fit regime, our body starts to remember the stretches, the lifts, the poses or distance running. If anyone has ever done yoga, remember how long it took to feel comfortable doing the 'downward dog'! This is when you are on your hands and feet, with bottom in the air. When you practised it more, the pose became more familiar to you and your body, making it easier to do.

When building physical muscles, the muscles are placed under stress. This causes micro tears that take place as you work out, which need time afterwards to repair and heal, stronger than before. The body also needs the right protein, rest and recuperation for this to happen.

Mental, emotional and spiritual fitness

This is the same as building physical muscles. Life is full of challenges and stress, but having the right tools alongside trust, faith, belief, hope and a greater percentage of positive thoughts than negative ones, we too can rest, repair and grow stronger. We can renew our brain and neural pathways to create new thoughts, changing how we think about ourselves and our world, and therefore how we feel.

Challenges such as dealing with success, loss, changes of circumstance or tough situations with family can knock us for six. However once we discover our thought patterns, our fallback position, we can change them for the better as necessary. Some of us can cope very well with job loss, for example, whereas for others it can be devastating. So we can start to work on the areas that are individual and important to us.

Once we learn how to handle situations, this builds muscle memory and our brain/mind, body, soul and spirit remembers how to manage and bounce back when trauma and/or drama happens again. Just like we can lose body weight, we can lose the old baggage, methods or thought processes that no longer serve us as we learn and grow in life. As we go through the different seasons of our life, we are forever learning and growing; none of us have it all together all of the time and we all have more to learn. This learning is not 'at all costs' though, as with too much to deal with, we can literally have a breakdown in whatever context that could mean; from bowing out of life to not being able to get out of bed and function on a daily basis, to functioning but with a certain numbness, i.e. taking on too much at one time without having an outlet. Like some body builders, we all know people who are over puffed in one area of life, such as their ego, job or fake happiness, and under developed in another, such as a rich family life or relationships. So growth and learning shouldn't be to the detriment of the things that are important to us such as our family or our health.

How life muscles benefit us

Building life muscles can help us to:

- Stay rooted, grounded and balanced
- Improve mental health
- Build emotional stamina and our ability to cope
- Improve resilience and build on inner strength
- Enhance the ability to defy adversity and to climb in life
- Increase the drive to succeed
- Deal effectively with difficulties with enough cushion to soften the blows
- Toughen up and have the energy to go on
- Improve our ability to think clearly
- Be able to adapt and cope with loss, success or other major changes of life

- Bounce back without bitterness and resentfulness
- Not only survive but thrive, grow and expand
- Rise up and blossom in life
- Recall good memories, 'memory capsules' when we need to draw upon them.

When we practise every day how to be resilient, how to manage life situations, to adapt, be flexible and pivot in life, we come to realise how powerful and strong we really are. We realise that we CAN cope, that there ARE rainbows in the sky, and we find that silver lining, if only we look for it, while building our minds, bodies and heart muscles to cope better.

Rather than being in a fearful state of mind that 'something bad is going to happen', we can remain in a state of readiness and preparedness, like 'life happens, but I'm going to enjoy it while dealing with all this stuff.' It is the realisation that there will always be 'stuff' to deal with, but as long as we are breathing and finding ways to handle it all, this will help us, our families and others around us.

Once you start working on yourself, you will realise how life aligns itself. How you think affects your feelings, which in turn affects what you attract and allows for enhanced synchronicity. This is the simultaneous occurrence of events which can make us pay attention to what we deeply desire or secretly ask for, as needs are suddenly met, people turn up or disappear and things come together almost perfectly.

For example, suddenly that job opportunity comes along, someone shows you their true colours, your partner shows up, whether physically or emotionally, or you see the book that you need to read. It also means being still enough to allow the Universe to line it all up for you.

'Trust the Universe has your Back'.

At this stage you may have to leave some people behind as you go forward on your journey, as not everyone will enjoy your new growth and/or state of independence.

Of course, we can also stay where we are in life, if it serves us and others well. Not everything is about change and it is okay to resist a life upgrade. However, you may find that life will, with its own sense of humour, put us into another situation to see if we'll learn, grow, do better and be better. Often, we still don't and we find ourselves repeating patterns and going around in circles, like 'hold on, I've been here before'. The danger is, like a pond with no fresh water source, we may start to stagnate and say 'well, this is just me'.

Staying in our comfort zone means we survive, stay safe and do very well thank you. That is perfectly okay. However, if you want to break any cycles or to jump out and do or think something different, then jump! This doesn't necessarily mean jump out of your whole life because there are always others involved, but it does mean you recognise that something needs to change if you are going to progress.

Also, if we always need to be busy or on the move and are never content, then that's another story. As humans, it's like we have an automatic switch to restlessness, or maybe the westernised world has created this state to match the consumption levels they want us to have: to constantly escape, travel, have experiences and buy, buy, buy. These things are nice… but will they ever feed the spirit?

The highest transformation is not external; it is internal. It is how much we love, share and uplift ourselves, our people, our village, our world. We are the change we want to see. Building life muscles will help us to make that change and this is why we need them.

Chapter 2
The Building Life Muscles Program

STOP. BREATHE. RESET.

Simple eh?

So what do we mean?

When building life muscles during challenging times, it is very easy to feel overwhelmed with what is actually happening, so we sometimes go into action mode rather than taking a moment to Stop and Breathe. In fact, it may feel safe to keep moving, that way we don't have to face our feelings. When we have had a shock of losing someone, maybe it is a small blessing in disguise to have to arrange a funeral; we keep busy, as we don't know how to process all the feelings at such a time. When we do come to breathe it is okay to take our time. It is acceptable to Stop and Breathe.

There is no good or bad way as sometimes it is what it is, when it is. Sometimes we need to go into dark areas to skulk when we are no good for anyone because we are going through some 'stuff'.

When going through challenging life situations it is important to:

- Keep it in perspective
- Look at the great and good things that have happened in your life by tapping into that memory capsule©
- Find solutions

- Start creating what you CAN be in control of
- Assess your whole life to see what you CAN do.

When we STOP it gives us a chance to BREATHE and RESET ourselves before we carry on.

STOP.
To check in with ourselves: our thoughts, our reactions, our emotions and our lives.

BREATHE.
To pause: to reflect and infuse our mind and body with oxygen for optimal performance.

RESET.
To recognise our fallback position: our natural thought processes and reactions so we can:

- Replace them if needed
- Recharge ourselves
- Reach out to others (with more energy) or reach out for further help
- Regulate ourselves to Stop, Breathe and Reset whenever we need to.

Every ten seconds we consciously or subconsciously make a mini choice about our state of mind and the many things that may be on our mind at any one time. It builds mind muscle memory for good, bad or indifferent. We make mini choices on how we want our life to go, how we react, what thoughts go over and over in our heads, who we want in our lives and more. Every time we make a mini choice to choose to change, to 'do better and be better', we build a life muscle.

If we stop for even 16 minutes a day of quiet (no phone or TV), a time to daydream and clean our thinking in order to refocus, re-imagine, reframe and reset, we have a chance to consciously unhinge ourselves from our past experiences and traumas. We have a chance to retrain and replace the neural pathways in our brain, to do the housekeeping on the brain and build life muscles to work for us and not against us.

However, we need to consciously do this Stop – 16 minutes for at least 21 days for the mind to replace thoughts, another 21 days to detox the mind/body and another 21 days to recharge and rebuild/replenish spirit, continually regulating by asking ourselves questions such as, 'What makes me think that?' or 'Why am I reacting like that?'

It may sound like a lot of days but if we have ever done a countdown to a big event, like a wedding, holiday or been on an exercise regime for three months to a year, it is the same concept. We can do the same for ourselves mentally, emotionally and spiritually by following this powerful, life changing Building Life Muscles program.

Try this exercise:

Take a breather

This section will help to bring you into the present moment, to relax the mind and body, improving your mental and emotional state of mind and bringing calmness. This will give your body a chance to de-stress, bring down blood pressure and flight or fight syndrome, and tell your brain to

release built up tension to let it all go.
Literally stop for a while and allow your shoulders to drop, allowing your breathing to become slower, allowing your mind to catch up to your here and now. If you find it hard to stop due to spiralling thoughts, physically stamp your feet or shout out STOP as a physical reminder.

If you are ready, let's do a 16 – minute pause right now. Sit back or lie down and see how it feels to be still and do nothing. Close your eyes and just allow your thoughts to wander, checking in on where you are at or what you have been processing lately.

Check in and recognise how your body feels… ask yourself why it feels that way? Is it a lack of sleep, exercise, great eating or mindset today?

And BREATHE… recognise your surroundings, your environment and be at ease with yourself and nature, allowing the muscles in your face to drop. Allow any tension or areas of the body you recognised that need to let go of emotional pain and/or stress. Allow yourself to become so peaceful, gentle and calm.

There's no need to do anything right now in this minute, as you let some minutes go by. Become aware of your breathing, so slow and gentle. On each outward breath, allow your body to drop even further into comfort, bringing in oneness with yourself, a soothing energy. On the slow exhale, you can even make gentle noises at the back of your throat to help you move out any energy not good for you. It could come out like a groan, low moan or simply 'whoosh' like a pressure cooker, letting out its steam.

Inhale positive thoughts / words, exhale out any negative ones and replace with positive ones from your memory capsule.
Only come back to the here and now when you are ready, opening your eyes in a calm, peaceful state, feeling recharged both physically, mentally, emotionally and spiritually.

How did you find that?

INSIGHT

Identifying a reset – Karen

When I tried this at home during the working week, I became twitchy and started planning in my head what I'm going to do in the next hour or day. Straight away but with discipline, each time I brought it back to my breath, my body, to the here and now and how I felt. After seven minutes or so, my thoughts started to unravel and my body started to relax more. My mind became clearer and I replaced random thoughts, issues and problems, with creative solutions coming to the fore of my mind. I started bringing people to my mind who I'm keen to reach out to and family members I need to touch base with. I ended up less twitchy and more in the now, with more breath in my mind, body and brain; thus improving my focus, energy and attention onto things which really mattered. That, I realised was a reset.

* * * * * *

Life can be like that, when we are going so fast that we forget to stop and appreciate what we have, who we have around us or what we are doing, until life sometimes forces us to stop. Imagine you are in a car moving at 70mph, what you see and experience outside the window becomes a blur as you are travelling very fast. Now imagine a parked car, a picnic or photo opportunity where we can take time to be in our surroundings and take it all in.

STOP. BREATHE. RESET.

Building life muscles while we Stop. Breathe. Reset means we get a chance to change how we work, change how we live our lives and change our thoughts around how we live with our family and friends. We get to create thoughts that serve us well, to consciously stop doing the things hurting us or someone else.

As we go through these thoughts and any changes it may help us to:

- Write it down, so it is out of our heads
- Talk to someone
- Have a 'silent scream' or real one into a pillow to rid yourself of frustration
- Do mindfulness colouring, drawing, sewing, gardening, something creative with your hands to give your mind a rest while you process everything

- Exercise physically to change our mental state and be able to take a breather.

Teachment©
We call these times 'contemplating your navel'. A time to gaze into oneself, to recalibrate, recharge and regulate the most expensive 'machine' you will ever own… yourself.

The following exercises can help you to ask yourself questions, assess where you are at and have a conversation with yourself. It will help to practically embed the Building Life Muscles program, to Stop. Breathe. Reset.

STOP. BREATHE. Let's check in with ourselves.

WORKSHEET – Exercise 1

How is my life today?
Look over these areas of your life and tick which box applies. Not how you would like it to be, but how you really feel it really is right now, this minute. Add any more areas you feel you need to. You can do this exercise any time you feel like it, or follow the guidelines in Chapter 3.

Areas of life	Great	Good	Okay	Needs some work	Overhaul needed
Mindset:					
Mental health and well being					
Money					
Work/Career/Business					
Body:					
Exercise routine					
General physical health					
Soul:					
Relationship with yourself					
Relationship with partner					
Relationship with family					
Relationship with friends					
Spirit:					
Inner peace and well being					
Faith					
Other (fill in yourself):					

Now write down three changes you would like to make in any of the different areas.

WORKSHEET – Exercise 2

How have I been coping?

Add your own life events: big, small, traumatic, meaningful or otherwise. Think of any events that impacted your thinking, lifestyle or way of life.

Life events	How did I cope then?	What would I do differently?	What have I learned? (the life muscles I have built)
Example: *Money habits*	*Spent £1000's without having anything tangible to show for it*	*Save more, buy property or some other tangible asset to have something to show for it*	*Utilise the here and now, take chances, use the system, use long term thinking rather than short term gain*
e.g. Wedding			
Lost job			
Divorced			

Continue on further pieces of paper as it can be quite cathartic to reflect, accept and learn from our past. If you need to talk it through, find someone you trust and/or a professional who will listen. There are further references and help at the end of this book.

WORKSHEET – Exercise 3

Who Am I?

If someone asked you this question, what would you say? Would you say, 'I'm a teacher, nurse, gardener, MP or banker' or would you say, 'I am a successful nurse and brilliant father'? Does your work define who you are? Who do YOU say you are? What are some of the words and thoughts that go through your mind on a daily basis? If they are negative, what would you prefer to say?

I am...	e.g. a mother worthy of love, I am loved, fun, kind, helpful, a success, a man of substance (fill in the blanks)
I am	
I am	
I am	
I am	
I am	
I am	

These can become part of your daily affirmations: this is where you can look in the mirror every day and say positive things to yourself, or throughout the day when you may need a 'pick me up'. The more you say them, the more they become a part of your life and belief system.

If you find yourself struggling to come up with nice words, why is that? Whose voice is that in your head? We will cover more of this as we go into parts Two, Three and Four of this book, but this is where self awareness brings knowledge, thus giving us the choice to change the negative into positive. This is where we reset.

RESET

Let's recognise our fallback position: natural thoughts, reactions and processes.

Recognising ourselves will give us more self-awareness about who we are and why we may do the things we do, in the way we do them, as well as identifying our natural reaction. Once we recognise our natural reaction, we can choose to do something about it if necessary. We can choose to Stop. Breath. Reset, as we take on the learning and build life muscles.

There is deeper work which can be done to discover who we are as a person, what makes us tick, what is our 'fall back' position: our emotional response to life situations, which will help us to work on how we reset: how we wish to not just react in the same way all the time but respond in a way that serves us. If our fallback position no longer serves us, we can consciously choose to change.

We all have certain triggers whether they are words, pictures, smells or sounds. We all have a certain piece of music which always catapults us to a happy or sad memory. This is our fallback position.

Now we are going to look at what our usual fallback or reaction is, especially when we are stressed. These tend to come out thick and sharp to whoever is around us, including ourselves. It is in that moment when we can make a mini choice as to what we do with those triggered thoughts or feelings.

We can use those times to let go of any bad memories and let them wash through us, so we are not stopping or rejecting the feeling. The thoughts that come after and what we do with them in word or action, is the most important moment of choice.

We can also use these times to put the good thoughts and feelings into a lovely memory capsule, so we can revisit them at any time. Matching a great memory with a sound, music or scent is a great way to bring that memory back.

WORKSHEET – Exercise 4

So, what has been your fallback position?
Think about your life and some of the recurring issues or moments where you tend to always think the same thing: good or bad, great or small. We have added some examples but try and add your own as a means of self-discovery and awareness.

Trigger	Fall back – Automatic Thought	Reset – Replace with a new Thought or Positive Affirmation, Word or Action
Examples: Made a mistake at work	I'm going to get fired or shouted at	I'll just sort it out then talk to my manager. It will be fine
Smells remind me of…	Missing my Mum – disappointment, anger, fear, abandonment, life is cruel	Life can be cruel but I have great memories, it is not happening right now, I release it, it's going to be okay
….		
….		
….		

Be honest with yourself throughout.

Spend as long as you need on this exercise, and use a separate piece of paper if you need to write more. Also come back to it as a reference point if you realise later on that you are constantly going back to a fallback position and you want to reset it. Spend some time in the reset area to see how you can replace your thoughts.

As we said before, it can take 21 days of constant resetting to embed a new habit or pattern; but for it to be embedded in our brain neural patterns as new thought behaviour can take up to 63 days. So keep going!

All four exercises can be incorporated into the daily, weekly and monthly 'checking in' with yourself.

Stop. Breathe. Reset.

Chapter 3

How to make the Life Muscles program work for you

We can start each morning with Stop. Breathe. Reset, or at any time during the day when you feel like you need an injection of strength to keep your mind on track with building life muscles.

Do what feels right for you on any given day, month or time of year.

DAILY SUGGESTIONS

1 - minute Anytime micro choice HIT

STOP.
Check in. Who am I? (Exercise 3)

BREATHE.
Pause. Take 5 deep long breaths. Bring up a nice memory from your memory capsule

RESET.
What has been my fallback position on a current issue? How can I replace that thought?

16 minutes – Morning mini choice

STOP.

Check in. How is my life today?
Who am I? (Exercises 1 & 3)

BREATHE.

Pause. Take 10 deep long breaths. Breathe out any cobwebs and bad dreams and breathe in the new beginning, new possibilities.

RESET.

What has been my fallback position on one issue today? (Exercise 4)

Replace negative thoughts with positive ones.
Say your affirmation

Recharge by saying 'YES' to life today.
Tell yourself 'I'm ready for today.'

Reach out. Think about those you might talk to today

Regulate your thoughts throughout the day, and come back to this space if triggered.

16 minutes – Night time mini choice

STOP.

Check in. How have I been coping today? (Exercise 2)
How is my life today? (Exercise 1)

BREATHE.

Pause. Breathe out any bad or frustrating moments throughout the day, let it go. Breathe in peace and thankfulness for all the good you have done today and all the people you have around you.

RESET.

What has been my fallback position on any issue today? (Exercise 4)

Replace negative thoughts with positive ones. Say your affirmation

Recharge saying 'THANK YOU' for the life you had today. Tell yourself 'I'm ready to recharge by sleeping well.' Hold onto the good things and put them into your memory capsule.

Reach out in kind thought to those who come across your mind.

Regulate your thoughts with affirmations as you drift off to sleep.

WEEKLY SUGGESTIONS

	Reminder to…	Action
Monday	Reset	Write down three good things that happened over the weekend that can help carry you into this new week. If not a great weekend, bring up a memory capsule. Go over your trigger and fallback list (Exercise 4), to remind yourself how best to reset. Add any more that come to mind. Stop. Breathe. Reset
Tuesday	Replace	Find two more solutions for any issues or problems you may be having (look over your fallback list from Monday) Use your goal list from Sunday to take action towards them. Start with one thing. Use positive affirmations to replace any negative words or thoughts
Wednesday	Recharge	Name one thing that has made you feel happy this week? Use that to feel the emotions for a minute... feel the feelings. What was so good about it? Add it to your memory capsule. What other goals can you action this week that will make you feel good?
Thursday	Reach out	Write down five people to be grateful for Name three people to touch base with this week Write down one person's name to forgive

Friday	Regulate	Review how this week went. How have I been coping? (Exercise 2) What uplifting word or sentence can describe it?
Saturday	Stop	Over breakfast or brunch, check in with yourself What three things went well this week? What three things were challenging? How could I 'do better, be better'?
Sunday	Breathe	Time to 'contemplate your navel' for 16 mins. Deep breath in…and out… Name ten things you are grateful for right now? Who am I? (Exercise 3) Set some goals for the week.
Any day bonuses		What can I do that will make me laugh today? What three things do I love about my life right now? Who can I appreciate today?

MONTHLY CHECK IN

Check in on where you are at now and make small choices, regulating how you want your life to be.	Go back to: Fallback and reset position (Exercise 4) Write down any more triggers that you have discovered and write down your reset word, affirmation or action. Redo the exercise 'How is my life today?' (Exercise 1)

QUARTERLY CHECK IN

Go to Seasons of Life (Chapter 9) and think about which season you are in now.	What life muscles can you put to use or build up for this stage of your life? Write down three positive affirmations. Write down three goals. Write down three action points towards each of your goals.

YEARLY CHECK IN

Time to jump on the scales of life and check in to make big choices for how you want your life to be.	Go back to the Exercises: How is my life today? (Exercise 1) How have I been coping? (Exercise 2) Who am I? (Exercise 3) What has been my fallback position in the different areas of my life? (Exercise 4) For the different areas of your life that need some attention, write down three goals for any changes you would like to make. Now write down three action steps towards each of your goals that you can take to get yourself there.

PART TWO
Stay Rooted

Stay rooted, grounded and balanced

Staying rooted, like a tree, means to be established, firm, solid and unshakeable, especially during challenging times in life. It can be great to be immoveable, but the irony is that we also need to be flexible and adaptable, so when the wind blows, we don't snap.

Chapter 4

THE BODY – Building Physical Life Muscles

When building physical muscles, the body remembers certain poses, stretches and positions, but it takes practice. It takes being aware of our body, what it is doing and what it is telling us. It is important to listen to the body, to understand its connection to emotion but also to treat the body with respect and look after it.

One way to respect the body is to build body strength. This includes things like lifting weights, using body weight when exercising, hill climbing and long walks.

Building body strength is important and can help us to build physical muscles, which in turn helps with:

- Flexibility and mobility
- Muscle size thus the power to charge, run and walk
- Endurance levels
- Preventing falls
- The ability to perform everyday tasks
- Slowing the rate of bone and muscle loss associated with ageing
- Improving our posture
- Reducing aches and pains
- Lowering the risk of injury.

Regular exercise ensures our body 'uses it, rather than loses it' until our body craves the endorphins' feel good factor that are released.

Listen to your body

When the body is in physical pain, it is trying to tell us that something is not right, physically, emotionally or even spiritually. The brain registers the pain we feel. Groaning or taking tablets is a distraction from the pain. This is fine, however, if we deny the registration of the pain, we deny the message our body is giving us; that there could be something drastically wrong. If something doesn't feel right, our body talks to us, we feel it in our gut and need to make a conscious choice about what to do next.

Men especially struggle to listen and go to the doctor. According to healthline.com, nearly two thirds of men avoid going to the doctors for as long as possible, and 37 per cent withhold information from their doctors. This can, of course, prevent doctors from detecting life-threatening issues early on, such as diabetes and high blood pressure (which can lead to strokes) and also cancer, including prostate cancer, traditionally found high in Afro Caribbean men. One friend only had it detected very early on because he utilised his private health plan yearly check and soon discovered how many men in his family had the same diagnosis, not all of them pulling through. How important it is then to share family medical history, to break down the silence, feel the vulnerability and talk to each other about our health.

Body – pain associations

Pain can also be a signal for emotional needs. When it happens, it could help if we identify:

- Which part of our body is in pain or uncomfortable?
- What is happening in our mind at the time?
- Are we stressed?
- Do we need to change our diet?
- Are we over worrying or taking on too much of a burden?

The book You Can Heal Your Life by Louise Hay often talks about what is going on in the whole of our lives at the time, which could help to explain the pain (bar any medical issues).

For example:

- Back issues could represent feeling unsupported, unstable and unloved
- Hip pain could be about the fear of moving forward, fear of making major decisions, thinking that there is nothing to look forward to
- Lower Back pain could represent anger. If you sit on frustration, the lower back is a common place for storing repressed anger
- Stomach and Intestines: Fear
- Heart and Chest: Hurt
- Headache: Loss of Control
- Neck /Shoulder Tension: Burdens and Responsibilities
- Fatigue: Resentments
- Numbness: Trauma
- Breathing Difficulties: Anxiety.

Look up www.alchemyofhealing.com to see if anything resonates with you. If you need to talk to someone, find a counsellor using BACP (British Association for Counselling and Psychotherapy). Find a therapist you click with, to discuss and explore any underlying emotional issues.

If you feel dis-ease, that something is not right, again it is a signal to take notice. What shows up in our body can be an indirect connection to an emotion, feeling or thought, which in turn can trigger a physical symptom. All physical experiences are of course very real, but how much of it can we help ourselves with?

INSIGHT

Shoulder pain and releasing the burden – Karen

A few years back, shoulder pain was common for me in the thick of being in the work 'engine room' to enable this 'big ship' to function, working 12 to 14 hours daily. I thought it was just my positioning at the desk, but I discovered by reading further that shoulder pain is aligned with burden. I realised I was resentful of carrying so much burden of all the businesses, and my work ethic meant I tried to leave no stone unturned. I was playing the martyrdom card again. Once I 'accidently' confessed this in one of our group reiki sessions, it helped to release the emotion behind the pain. I decided to let it go. This, along with swimming and massage, I believe helped to unlock muscle ache and trauma from my body before it manifested long-term physical damage.

*   *   *   *   *   *

Dealing with daily physical pain

Deep down inside of us we have the ability to allow that pain to flow through us, rather than to come in and stay with us. Just like when it's a cold day, if we resist the cold, we feel colder but if we allow it to flow through us to become part of that coldness, we don't feel it as much. So, breathe in deeply and out, releasing tenseness in the body. Stop. Breathe. Reset.

Sometimes it's good to have something to distract us, to laugh or reminisce about good times, or to just focus on a game or something we are genuinely interested in. Some people tap their fingers as a distraction, or hum, rock, or groan; these are also useful ways to distract the brain to ease the pain. If the pain becomes our focus, it becomes our sharp painful reality.

It may seem impossible, especially when recovering from an operation, but sitting outside or going for a walk in nature, gardening, swimming and dancing can be good for us. Apart from encouraging mindfulness and being in the moment, it helps us to relax, which in turn can help to reduce pain. Not everyone has the ability to access this, but we can always ask for help from our GP, our family or friends.

Loss of health

A loss of power and strength in the body can be exhausting, especially when dealing with additional and unexpected illnesses such as Long Covid. To have to deal with pain daily slows down our life, and can change who we are as a person. We may feel unrecognisable and like we are a burden to others, when we have to rely on them for help.

One person's story - BD

Everyone's experiences of misfortune are unique. The reason for misfortune can look the same, but living through the experience of the cause of pain, grief and loss, and its aftermath, is solely unique to that person. Many people have had major surgical procedures; but what I will reflect on is my experience of it and how, through the pain, the confusion, the fear and uncertainty, there has been a thick growth of love and belief that has surrounded me, maintained my sense of self and wellbeing and, even in the darkest moments of self-doubt, anger and panic, kept me cushioned and feeling held until the fear passed.

When we think of hospitals, and we think of pain, we generally envisage a person in physical pain. However, there is also the emotional pain that is experienced. What is more, there is the pain that loved ones go through. Because my stay in hospital took place during Covid-19, I was not allowed any visitors. No one was allowed to stay with me in the ward. Being isolated was one of the most painful effects of being in hospital. The sense of solitude was not only about being alone but also about not having the touch of a loved one. This meant dealing with feelings of loss and fear on my own.

I have always known that the experiences we have in life can, when we pay attention, help us learn from the mistakes and the successes; to help us to deal with other situations we come across. What I am beginning to understand during this healing process is that some situations are so different, so unusual that we do not have the wherewithal to cope with them. This is when we need help: help to reach out and find the courage, the strength, the knowledge, the encouragement, and the faith to keep the panic at bay.

This reflection concerns a situation I find myself in. It is an experience that concerns my whole self. It concerns not only my physical, but also my psychological, emotional, and spiritual sense of wellbeing. It is a case where my very life was at risk due to an undiscovered medical issue, and what began with an almost benign preliminary diagnosis morphed into something requiring a major medical procedure. One of the first things I reflected on, when I was compos mentis enough to string whole thoughts together, was 'what the hell just happened?'

This particular journey began while the country, and the wider world was beginning to settle into life with the threat of Covid 19, and struggling to make the necessary adjustments to their everyday lives, in line with government and medical guidelines, to keep safe and not contract the virus. For me this was trying hard to keep working, to keep researching and writing, with regular breaks for exercise and daily walks outdoors.

Several months prior to the pandemic I was diagnosed as having costochondritis by my doctor. Costochondritis is inflammation of the muscles where the ribs join the breastbone. The main symptom of costochondritis is sharp chest pain that is worse when moving and breathing. I did not have severe symptoms, the pain was relatively manageable, so treatment was not thought necessary. However, it was during one of my walks with my husband that the pain flared up to such a degree we had to cut short the walk and come home. The pain increased and after careful consideration, given the situation with hospitals and the Covid 19 virus, I took the decision to dial 999 and call an ambulance.

From there the situation slipped into a series of tests being conducted. The diagnosis of costochondritis was upheld and I had one foot out of the door of the casualty department when I was told there was a final 'just in case' test that had been done, and the doctors were waiting for the result before they felt I could be discharged. When the results came in everything became a whirl. I was admitted and several days later had a major operation which involved what one doctor described as a 'brutal' procedure to save my life.

The question of what the hell happened is one that I am currently working through. I am very slowly piecing together the events of my stay in the hospital. What I am not doing is piecing together the events surrounding the actual procedure because I am scared. Right now, I do not need to look at what was taken out, moved or replaced, nor how many machines I was plugged into in order to keep me alive. No, what I need to know is why, how and what it all means. What did my body do that enabled it to survive?

The biggest question of all is existential: what does this mean for me? My life was threatened and through the knowledge of experts and surgeons, I endured a procedure that has left its scars on my body and on my spiritual and psychological self. I am left with post-traumatic stress (PTSD) symptoms, which the medical profession still often fails to recognise in patients who have experienced major surgical procedures. In truth, patients fail to recognise it in themselves.

The symptoms of post-traumatic stress are many and varied but include flashbacks, hypervigilance, anxiety and emotional distress. Sound familiar? For me, these symptoms were remarkably familiar. I have spent decades in private practice as a psychotherapist, and during those years have encountered clients whose past experiences engendered PTSD and who lived with the symptoms every day. For many people, these feelings were categorised as everyday stress.

Stress is a word that we have in our vocabulary and we use it to describe a variety of symptoms that people experience caused by an equally diverse set of misfortunes and circumstances. It may be a person is working too hard, or is struggling with finances, or is suffering from burnout caused by high expectations from managers at work. Equally people suffer when they have high expectations of themselves as a result of being high achievers. It could be caused by personal relationships, or illness or a loss in the family. Sometimes it can be a disturbing experience that leaves certain feelings resurfacing from time to time. Such stress can lead to feelings of anger, resentment, or feeling low or depressed. Now I find myself amongst those people struggling to make sense of what happened to them.

One way was to use what I did know and had learned throughout my working years as well as connecting with others who were also in recovery, and to read and talk with experts and ask questions about my recovery. During those times when we are in the greatest need, we often forget that within ourselves we have a wealth of knowledge and experience that can serve to provide a means to begin to take steps to healing and recovery.

I wish to leave this brief reflection with these words; I have no idea where I am going, I do not see the road ahead of me, I cannot know for certain where it will end nor do I really know myself, and the fact that I think I am following my path does not mean I am actually doing it. But I believe the fact that I have hope and desire in all I am doing, keeps in hope that I will never do anything apart from that desire, and I know that if I do, I will lead myself on the right road though I may not know anything about it. Therefore, I will trust in myself though I may seem to be lost and, in the shadow, I will not fear, because I am filled with love and care. I will never be left to face my perils alone.

Whether it may be a doctor, a nurse, a family, a friend, a priest or your Goddess or God, there will be love surrounding you during your healing. I wish you a good journey.

Be honest with yourself

Do you want to stay in your pain?

Counter intuitive as it sounds, in our experience, some people hold onto pain because it is all they know and it feels comfortable.

There is a safety in pain when we don't know how to handle life or we are not ready to face certain truths, and there can be a dissonance without it. That's okay.

Whether it is physical or emotional, it can, however, become our only story. The story that we tell anyone who will listen and everyone we meet, all the time until it becomes a way of life, a state of mind.

Is your pain eating you up and affecting your mood, and therefore everyone else's mood? Of course the pain is real and some of us need real medicine, but have we ever told the pain that 'you can go away now I no longer need you?'

Or is the pain intricately linked to our emotion and thoughts about someone, what they did or didn't do, said or didn't say? Is it time to forgive them, so we can let love seep through us to let it go?

Of course it's easier said than done, but look how much we could share with someone else going through what we did, if we can overcome this phase of our lives. How many other people could be helped by listening to how we got through the 'eye of the needle?'

Have faith

Have faith in the ability of the body, which has an amazing inner navigating system to guide and help us when we need it. We as human beings have a natural program, which helps to keep the body alive, alerting us of any danger as we cling to survive. The challenge is how to listen, and also how to incorporate faith, belief and trust that all will be well. We don't always know what 'well' means as some of our loved ones don't stay alive or physically well 100 per cent. However in the midst of it all, to be able to calm our mind we can tell ourselves, it is still well. This way we stay thriving for as long we can, as best we can, to enrich our lives and also the lives of others.

INSIGHT

One Energy systems and the power of intent – Devon

I think I have an advantage because I practise One Energy systems of healing, which provide an understanding about using the energy around our own thoughts and the power that goes into the intent. If you put out there that you want to heal yourself and/or others, this is what you will reap. The body and life have its own momentum and it doesn't always end 'well' in our minds, but intention helps the process. It also helps doctors and nurses to help you. The healing starts with 'I am… I want to'. It is using these thoughts to replace negative ones.

* * * * * *

Focus on something positive

It can be useful to have a goal or reward, something to look forward to, to strive for in the future, so that every step is a step closer to our goals. Whether it's the ability to be able to walk again or be strong enough to move around, let us try to convince our brain to strive for that target to gain independence. Even the smallest movements can give us a sense of achievement, rather than looking at the whole picture at that stage. After all, we wouldn't expect to eat our dinner in one bite, it is always a small portion at a time, but we still reach the end of our meal.

Teachment©

Lean on who you need to during those tough times, to help hold you up, keep the faith and keep going. Life may look totally different than it was before, but with a level of acceptance as well as determination, see what you CAN control and take charge of the narrative of your life as best you can.

Chapter 5
The MIND – Building Mental Life Muscles

What does it mean to have good mental life muscles?

It means developing good life habits, so we can adapt in the face of adversity, trauma, tragedy, threats and stress, not to just get through or function but to be able to:

- Accept life's disappointments
- Meet life's daily demands
- Make decisions with clarity
- Shape our own environment
- Feel good about ourselves
- Not be constantly overwhelmed by fear, anxiety, anger, jealousy, love or guilt
- Build lasting relationships
- Be comfortable with people
- Laugh at ourselves and at life
- Respect ourselves.

Mental strength involves our ability to feel, think and perform at our best.

Coping strategies

When we are ready to tap into our inner strength and develop more self-awareness, we can start to create our best life in order to:

- Stay positive
- Control anxiety
- Be able to visualise 'our best life'
- Be able to set goals

- Increase our ability to cope and know we have some controls in our hands
- Be able to take back control and set targets
- Create healthy habits
- See each challenge not as a threat but an opportunity
- Feel confident rather than unsettled.

We can develop ourselves from wherever we start from, no matter what our current learned behaviours, thoughts and actions.

Why, though, are we prone to defaulting to and believing negative thoughts, outcomes, news or words said about us?

We are built for survival like animals and are always on the lookout for danger, but surely after thousands of years we can evolve from the fight or flight system within us? Instead of a fallback position way of thinking, we can 'Stop, Breathe and Reset' to decide how we really want to think. We are intelligent human beings who can consciously change our thoughts at any time.

We do have another human side, which sometimes makes mistakes, but this can also teach us to build stronger life muscles. We can learn to:

- Build healthy self-talk
- Face fears head on
- Build character (morality, honesty, compassion, patience)
- Build on our gratitude
- Take personal responsibility.

It is okay to make mistakes and it is also okay to swing across the whole emotional pendulum in one day. Life will happen but it is how we react which is crucial and where we choose to stay in our heads and for how long. It is all about what happens in our thoughts.

Do we think we CAN, or do we think we can't?

'Whatever we think, so it is'.

Adaptation and flexibility

Elasticity of the mind is something we all have, giving us the ability to change, grow, extend, mutate, solve problems and overcome the neural and psychological barriers that can impede growth.

When there is something new happening in our lives, which is more often the case post pandemic, where our lives may not feel as secure, we could have the tendency to resist and stay inflexible. However one of the greatest tools we have is the ability to adapt.

No matter what we think we know, we are never too old to learn a new thing, to open our heart to compassion, to think differently, to retune our minds, to bend if we need to, otherwise life can break us. It can hold us down in a gridlock if we allow it. Surrendering to what is right now means we can manage this day. Then we can prepare for tomorrow but manage it tomorrow.

One thought / moment at a time

Climbing a mountain can be daunting at first, but concentrating on the one step in front of us means we can break down the seemingly insurmountable journey. When we achieve that step, we can take the next step, if we just look at what is right in front of us. Let us just try, without a timeline if necessary. If we don't complete it today, then let us carry on tomorrow. Be in that moment.

Stay rooted – ground your mind

It is very easy to allow whatever is happening in and around our lives to take centre stage and rule our day. Of course, the whole situation will be on our minds the whole time, even if we still manage to go to work or get the kids off to school.

It is up to us to keep it in perspective and acknowledge that while we may not have everything that we think we need right now, we still have what we've got. Beyond the issue, problem or concern, we have life, which is still something. We can still draw upon inner strength, even just a chink, by tapping into our mind and controlling our thoughts on a deeper subconscious level as well as our breath.

Use your subconscious mind

INSIGHT

A stream of consciousness – Devon

Where the mind goes.... our own record, playing in our heads all the time, without paying rent.... what is life? Life in my opinion is a perception. My life is my perception of my being. To succeed in my perception of my life, is to have a better understanding about me. What is my strength? What is my weakness? What are my likes and dislikes? Can I be honest to myself? What is it that I would like to achieve? What am I prepared to do to achieve my goals? So with that in mind how determined will I be to achieve my goal? Can I do things that I don't particularly want to do? Can I go to places that I don't want to go? Can I hear things that I don't want to hear and make it ok to reach my goal? Can I be in the company of people that I don't want to be with and make it ok? Can I take the loneliness of being so focussed on my goals? Yes I must, it's just for a while. If not, I will just be floating in the wind and it's just for a while, for me to achieve it is ok till I reach my goal.

We can think like this in seconds, no wonder our heads get so full. Imagine our subconscious mind and what it can process! We have thousands of thoughts every day. How do we manage these swirling thoughts?

'Stop. Breathe. Reset'. Refer to the Building Life Muscles program and do one of the 16-minute pause sessions.

Here is another way to look at our thoughts and why they are so powerful. Thought, Emotion, Action©

Let's Stop, Breathe… and have a cup of T.E.A.

T – Thought
E – Emotion
A – Action

When we have a thought that triggers an emotion (fallback), we get to decide what our action (reset) is going to be. We can keep going back to that emotion, bringing up all those feelings (which is fine) but we can also reset and create a new thought which will trigger different emotions which could serve us better.

Of course, this is easier said than done. Just like physical muscles take time and discipline to build, so the same goes for the mind. It takes conscious training.

We can remind ourselves to go back to the 16 minutes pause of 'contemplating our navel' to transform ourselves, one thought at a time.

*   *   *   *   *   *

INSIGHT

Overcoming frustrating emotions – Devon

When I used to stutter, my immediate thought was, 'they can't hear me, I can't say what I want to say'. I wanted to change how I felt. Why did I lash out? My primal instinct was to defend and lash out physically. The emotion was one of frustration, then regret which lowered my self-esteem. I didn't want to be taken the mickey out of anymore, so I decided to slow down and not talk as much, so I could be more in control of myself. I then felt relief to be heard at last, to have a full conversation. I realised I could change the way I spoke to have greater autonomy over the use of the spoken word. I changed how I spoke consciously by breathing, talking slower and with more conscious effort, so that my brain would slow down for my words to catch up. I had to control my breath, so thinking, then speaking. 'Stop. Breathe. Reset'.

*   *   *   *   *   *

Having a relationship with our mind first

Let us stop relying on our partner, friend or Mum to 'prop' us up. We need to stand on our own two feet. Yes, lean on them sometimes and of course ask for help but at the end of the day, no one is responsible for our happiness and contentment except us. It is way too much pressure to put that on someone else's shoulders.

In helping ourselves, we can become aware of the 'record' that plays in our head (our fallback). We may be playing the record of, 'I love myself', 'Look at you, you can't do that', 'You are dirty, nasty, ugly', 'Everyone is out to get me, she/he did it again' or 'I am my trauma, and this is my story'.

These thoughts are powerful and could derive from a combination of our nature, our DNA, generational thought patterns and behaviours, our nurture, our womb experience, our upbringing and our experiences.

We may have subconsciously given other people this power over us. When we become aware of this record and our thoughts, we can start to change and control the narrative ourselves. This is not easy, as we may have been told these lies many times or conjured up stories for ourselves in order to cope.

We can consciously change that power by turning down the volume dial on that negative voice and replacing it with our own truth, power, love and kindness to ourselves. If you need additional support with this, it is okay to get help from a professional. There may be setbacks when talking it through and it can feel worse before it feels better, as fresh and old emotions and wounds are uncovered. However it can become a powerful game changer for our lives and those around us as we transform. This is where elasticity of the mind works; it is new but doable.

Our thoughts affect us and also our families more than we think. Our energies, moods, ambition and thoughts all have an energy field that goes beyond ourselves. When we come across someone who our spirit 'just can't take to' or 'there is something about that person', they are giving off more than they are saying: they affect us.

Protecting our minds

Where are we sending our energy? Knowing how energy translates into everything we touch and feel, means that the food we eat, the liquids we drink, who we have around us,

what we listen to and what we watch all impacts our mind, body and soul.
In turn, we also affect others. People are watching us, especially children. They will soak up our energy and they learn how to handle any pain from our behaviours.

What do you want them to learn?

We can be in control of our thoughts and the direction of our thinking. It is quite easy to get carried away with what people say, their expectations, their agendas and what is perceived to be the norm.

The choice still remains with us to be positive or negative. It comes back to our willingness to let go of unhealthy thoughts and energies. It's always a great idea to fill our mind with positive images, sounds, actions, people, TV and podcasts, so that we stay in control of the narrative.

The thoughts we have can harm us or heal us. Staying in positive energy is not denying the dark but finding better coping mechanisms for life and light.

Endure and reboot the will to live

When things seem really dark, we can feel like we've had enough of life. The wanting to live has to come from within us. If we remember that we are the author of our lives, we can make it what we like. Think of the future.

Who is in your corner?

It could be your partner, children, parents, friends or colleagues, who are suffering with you but are hopefully helping you to recover.

We can then match their desire for us to recover… to do what is required to survive, knowing that us living impacts theirs lives as well. Having an inner circle of support, care and love means that sometimes it's others who help to carry us until we can stand up on our own two feet.

INSIGHT

Overcoming heartbreak – Karen

When I separated from my daughter's father, many moons ago, I was devastated. My Mum, Dad and sisters were there for me, and my daughter. I had to crush my she-go and ask Mum and Dad if I could move in temporarily. Little did I know how much that meant for my daughter, as she recalls precious memories, especially with my Mum but also my Dad as being a consistent male figure in her life. I felt ashamed to go back home, like a failure but while I recovered from heartbreak, financial upheaval, and worked and studied, they were my lifesavers. My daughter forced me, in my mind, to survive, live and thrive, otherwise I would have run away but I needed her to see me strong through the tears. I needed to make a better life for me and for her.

* * * * * *

Ways to ground our mind:

- Meditate
- Read or listen to uplifting books and stories
- Pray
- Do yoga or any exercise such as kickboxing and dancing, which are great ways to release strong emotions. Afterwards you could sit still and concentrate on the breath; stilling your mind, reassessing the whole situation.
- Be in your body, the 16-minute pause, breathing from your core, gaining strength, clarity and control over your mind and body again, to help calm nervousness and the feeling of overwhelm.
- Realise that you still have the power to re-imagine your life
- Have a cup of T.E.A©!

Take a breather…
Stop. Breathe. Reset.

Ground yourself by taking in your surroundings right now. Take a deep breath in for the count of six and out for the count of six, repeat as many times as you need to calm swirling thoughts.

What do you see around you?
What can you hear?
What can you touch?
What can you taste?
What do you feel?

Take another deep breath in for the count of six and out for the count of six and remain in that calm state, while you receive what you need to from this book.

Drawing on inner strength

We are stronger than we can ever imagine; all we need to do is to learn to dig deep into ourselves, to have the desire to do something enough. If we wait for someone to help us do something, we'll never come up with the right time to help ourselves. There is so much more power in knowing that we've achieved something for ourselves, as it makes the next obstacle easier to manage and overcome. There are going to be things we do not like, which make us feel uncomfortable but we can learn, we can put one foot in front of the other, one step at a time to help keep us going when we have the energy.

Feeling vulnerable is okay

Falling down is okay, when we run out of steam. Feeling powerless is okay. We may stay here for a while, in pain, with pain, traumatised… and that is okay.

We cannot hurry recovery; it takes place in its own time and place. Of course, mentally we can have some say in the matter, however we also know when it's time to draw the covers over our head, close the curtains and shut the world out for a while, to cope with it all.

Within that space, we can start drawing on that inner strength by resetting our thoughts, grounding ourselves and digging deep. We can Stop, be still and take time to centre ourselves. Be still enough to take stock, feel the feelings, let them come up, Breathe and let them flow out of our body as we breathe deeply and calm our body and our mind.

Then, after some time of restoration and recharge, we may need to Reset, to get up again, to reach out, as someone else may need our help. There is no one exactly like us, to do what we do, to share our experiences, in our small part of the world. Who knows what impact we may have on somebody, who knows how many more wonderful memories there are to create in our lives and in the lives of others.

We have such a wealth of knowledge and ability; we just sometimes lack belief. We don't need permission for this belief, or permission to engage in our inner strength. We just need to draw from it.

Take a breather

Think back to how you got through a hard time or if this is your first 'event', trust that you have the capacity to get through, to build life muscles, inner strength, the mechanisms and tools to use again and/or share with someone else.

Take in all the breath you need as you sigh through this time, dig deep into your soul and tell yourself, it will be okay, over and over until it feels like it. Then you make up your mind to get through another moment, minute by minute, day by day.

INSIGHT

Accepting unexpected events – Karen

When Devon was in hospital after a sudden pain in 2019, then unexpected major operation, I remember him saying, 'I wanted to walk and get out of bed by myself even when the physiotherapist came to help because I felt like I needed to test myself first. I didn't see myself as poorly as others, so I pushed myself to walk down the corridor. If you tried something and you weren't able, it is also not a bad thing. I had to dig deep, to when I was a boxer and footballer, to how I didn't like losing. It wasn't part of my vocabulary, as I always looked to see how I could do better. The physical pain from the recovery was immense, the mental pain was absolute, but the reward was phenomenal.'

It was very hard to accept anything in those moments in the hospital – to accept that life is out of our control sometimes. However, to keep going and un-tense my shoulders and heart, I had to keep telling myself, 'It is all going to be okay, regardless of the outcome'. Knowing that the universe always has our best interests at heart.

* * * * * *

Living in the uncomfortable zone

It's not you; it's me
Is it always someone else's fault or is it time to look at yourself yet?

Have you discovered that your anxiety or stress has nothing to do with your boss or your work colleague, but that it is all about you and your own thoughts?

Is there a new stress coming up from the relationships in your home or do you realise it's the same stresses and actually, the only thing in common is you?

This is where it can get uncomfortable.

The uncomfortable zone is scary

It is always important to remember that when we are making a transformation in our life, it is a new awakening. It is not going back to what was but a new way of being and thinking. If we try to go back to what was, we may be disappointed that it doesn't fit as comfortably as before.

The uncomfortable zone gives us a chance to transform and create the person we would like to be and the life or household we aspire to be in. It is giving us a chance to choose better or more every day, even in our thought pattern.

It means leaving behind old aspects of us that do not serve us anymore. It also means looking at people who should no longer be in the space we are moving into. People in our life matter, even if we need to move a bit away from them. Not everyone has to be within our inner circle. Recovery or renaissance can be a lonely place but it's always good to remember that the people around us are not on our journey and they are not going to the same place we are. We can still be together but we need to be on this journey.

Take a breather

Use whatever words you need to give yourself a pep talk when it feels uncomfortable. For example:

1) I got this
2) I can do It
3) It won't be like this forever
4) I need to move on.

If we have disengaged to go on this journey, we may feel like we are missing out on something when we are not in certain circles. However we can ask ourselves, what have I learned about myself, my past and my past perception of life?

Do I need to constantly surround myself with certain types of people if they drag me down, are always negative, make no room for me or make me feel small?

Step away from drama, as if we sow drama, it is easy to reap and attract. Sow dishonesty, it is also easy to reap that back into our life. Let us have our own root. Let us concentrate on ourselves, our business and our family. Which is not to say we can't help others, but not to the detriment of ourselves.

Teachment©

Your awakening happened for a reason and now you have a chance to decide who it is you want to be. Tell yourself you have the strength and ability to think it, intent it, say it and believe it. Then you have to walk the walk.

People, things, opportunities and dramas will keep popping up, which is life's uncanny way of checking in with us to see if we really want to move on, act differently or have a positive set of people in our lives. Life will test us to see what we are really made of, so building life muscles will enable you to stay rooted, grounded, firm and strong.

Living with uncertainty

Life is uncertain in the best of times, but particularly during the 2020 pandemic, life became uncertain almost on a daily basis. Not knowing if the outside world would ever be the same again, and not knowing if our jobs, our homes and our family would be safe, but most importantly our health.

No matter what the situation is, it will always be about how we react to the situation, rather than the situation itself. This determines how or if we handle it and how it affects us, and all those who come in contact with us, for the rest of our lives.

Tools to help us cope can include:

- Getting back to basics and just being grateful for food and shelter, if we have this
- Being aware of what we listen to and watch. There is so much information bombarding us, we need to filter what we allow into our realm of thought and imagination, so it does not lead us to expect the worst all the time
- Filling our minds with good thoughts
- Having a plan A but also a plan B, C and D so we

are not disappointed if it cannot happen in the way or timescale that we expect

- Taking regular breaks and remembering to call family and friends, sharing how we feel, so it's off our mind, especially if working in the isolation of our homes
- Using distractions such as comedy for laughter, mindful colouring, gardening and any other interests
- Keeping a gratitude journal for all the things which might be going okay in your life despite the uncertainty
- Doing exercise and self-care on a daily basis
- Using the grounding session in the earlier section 'Take a breather' to pause for a bit
- Using complementary therapies such as massage plus essential oils or naturopathic remedies to help us to manage and reset
- Asking for support from family, friends or a professional.

When we feel overwhelmed, here is a reminder of the things we can control in uncertain times:

- When we wake up
- When we go to bed
- How much exercise we do
- What we read
- What we watch
- When we wash
- The fun we have
- How we relax
- What we learn
- How tidy our space is

- If we write or journal
- Talking on the phone
- When we dance
- When we listen to music
- When we cook
- Reaching out to someone else in need
- Reaching our goals or at least planning them out and preparing.

Take a breather

Stop and allow yourself five minutes of worry and negativity, really go for it and think of all the worst things that could happen. Then come back to reality and see what is really happening.

Take a long deep breath, and remind yourself that:

'It is all happening perfectly right now this minute.'
'I am fine.'

Replace with your own words of affirmation and carry on. Use these words anytime you find yourself spiralling into worry and anxiety.

Maybe you can make your own list of what you CAN control.

Feeling a feeling and allowing it to flow through you

We are human beings not doers so it is okay for us to feel emotions. It is okay to say things like:

‘I feel angry’
‘I’m pissed off!’
‘I feel mad and desperate’
‘I feel like I hate her right now.’

Plus, it is okay for us to sit for a while in those feelings, either expressing them to someone else or just to ourselves, and really allowing ourselves to be real and feel the feelings.

This is the part where we are just honest with ourselves and acknowledge the truth of our feelings without judgement. There is no point covering them over with a plaster of positive thought unless we have to steel ourselves to go to work, or drop the kids or have caring duties. However, if we have the time, let us sit still to process our feelings.

Processing feelings is learning to understand, make sense of and deal with our emotions in a healthy and productive way. One way to acknowledge an emotion is to allow it to flow through us until it goes into ‘nothingness’, into the air: we have no more to give it, we are exhausted, thus dissipating its intensity. We can then release the emotion, saying ‘thank you’ and acknowledging that it is here for us to learn and grow.

Once this is done and it can happen often over the same issue (so we are not always fixed in a day or even a month or year), we can reflect on what triggered those strong emotions. We can realise our fallback position and choose to reset. We can rediscover parts of ourselves, parts of our memories, parts of us we may not want to see, which are nevertheless calling for us to deal with them.

We are not always ready to deal with what comes up, so if it is too much, you are in control of whether you put it back inside the 'no' box for another time. However, if the box keeps getting flung open, life is usually trying to teach us and is eager for us to heal and grow beyond what we feel we might be capable of. We may have asked for it, or life has more in store for us, and the people around us.

Putting our feelings and emotions into a box is like putting old hurts and pains away onto a shelf which may come down again, or maybe it is okay to stay up there for the rest of our lives. This is different from repressing our emotions, which may mean that we are trying to press them down when they want to come up, but we keep pressing them down anyway. Life knows we can handle dealing with these feelings but we sometimes fear them or lack confidence in our ability to manage.

Repressed emotions could make us feel:

1. Numb, lacking any emotion
2. Nervous when others share their feelings
3. In a low state, often without realising why
4. Stressed and experiencing undiagnosed aches and pains.

If this is the case, maybe we should talk to someone about it as soon as we feel able to. Repressed emotion can create toxicity in our body, mind and heart; its energy often gets stored in our body, organs, muscles and tissue. This can lead to inflammation, chronic health problems and affect our mental health and wellbeing.

To summarise, how do we allow the feelings to flow through us?

- Stop. Feel the feeling
- Acknowledge the feeling and name it, e.g. anger, jealousy, joy, peace
- Reflect on why those feelings have come up
- Say 'thank you' and release the feelings
- Rediscover parts of ourselves and reset – how do we really want to feel?
- Put any other parts of feeling you are not ready to deal with back in the box for now
- Reset your thoughts
- Breathe… and carry on.

Allowing the good times

When we have been through a traumatic time, being tense for so long, it can be very hard to know when we can allow our mind, body, soul and spirit to have fun again, to laugh, to dance, to feel good. Especially when we have experienced the passing of a loved one, we may feel like we are betraying the person – how can we be laughing and having fun, when that person is no longer with us?

Does it mean we have forgotten the person? Or does it mean we moved on and didn't need them in our lives in the first place or that they didn't mean as much to us as we thought they did? Does that mean the same will happen to us? This is something that is scary to even think about, that life will inevitably go on beyond our passing.

However, it is important to allow ourselves to feel happy. It is okay to draw on a good 'memory capsule' with that person and smile. It is okay for us to tell ourselves to be content, feel the joy, feel the peace, feel the fun and enjoy the laughter.

We may recognise some of these reasons why we may not enjoy the lovely times, fully and unapologetically:

- We are afraid the worst will happen
- We feel like it isn't deserved
- Feeling like it's too much work, it almost becomes stressful!
- We don't like to see other people enjoying themselves
- Feeling that it is hard to enjoy as there may be bad times just around the corner
- Feeling like 'happiness' needs to be controlled
- Feeling like other people's 'happiness' needs to be controlled.

It may be very obvious why we feel or react that way due to what people have done to us earlier in life. Or we may have allowed ourselves to get trapped into a fallback position without fully realising it. Revisiting the Stop. Breathe. Reset chapter can help us to develop more useful habits.

Building life muscles to allow the good times enables us to:

- Regulate our emotional responses: Stop, Breathe, Reset
- Rebalance and rein in the spiralling thoughts
- Be resilient and bounce back
- Bounce back without bitterness

- Rise up and choose to blossom in life
- Re-stimulate the good times by reintroducing playing, dancing, games or whatever you, your family or friends used to do
- Recall good memories from our 'memory capsules' when we need to draw upon them
- Just allow us to be in the moment, in the NOW.

Take a breather

Time for a Stop. Breathe and silent 16min Reset as we take time to breathe in for the count of six and breathe out for the count of six. Do this until you feel like you are back in your body: becoming aware of how each part of your body is feeling, being in the present, in the now.

Reviving the good times (scent, colours, sounds)

We can revisit positive memories at any time by applying markers to that great event or occasion using our senses, e.g. scent, visual, touch or sound. This way we start to build memory capsules©: pockets of memory we can revisit to comfort us at any time.

Scent

We can deliberately use scent in those good times to breathe in and anchor that time while it is happening; e.g. use a room spray, the cooking smells, a perfume or an essential oil on a tissue. Growing up, we may have had many cooking smells that mean roast dinner, curry time or a good Jamaican feast. It could be a nearby bread factory, flowers in a picnic field or an aftershave. Whatever it is, become more aware of these smells. Stop. Breathe. Reset to anchor that memory in a few seconds, by being in the here and now of the moment.

It even works when we are trying to study: basil or bergamot are good essential oils for concentration and a pick me up respectively.

To draw out these memory capsules©, just use the same or similar scent to remember those good times.

Visual

Create pictures on your phone, pick up postcards, pick up a plant, anything that you can see which will trigger great times and great memories. You can of course close your eyes and 'see' with your mind. Pausing to visualise can be even more powerful than the actual doing, just like athletes who envision themselves running and winning before they do it. The muscle memory from mind and body work well to make it naturally happen.

Touch

A piece of material, clothing or jewellery is a great way to help bring back a memory, to bring in a pause moment, to help ground us. We can touch it anywhere we are, to help remind us to ground ourselves, to breathe, to drop our shoulders and let go.

Sound

If you don't have a piece of music which you can play to remind you of good times, go back and play every piece of music you can, wherever you have it stored. Over the next month just play music every chance you get, and memories will probably start flooding back. Put aside the great memories to play when you need a pick me up.

If negative memories and emotions come up while going through some of these, allow them to wash through you, acknowledge them and see where they come from. Allow healing as necessary, allow yourself to reach out and talk to someone if this is what you need.

INSIGHT

Childhood aromas – Devon

In Jamaica, I remember as a child, I was always walking along the main coastal road, looking through a fence towards the beach where big people were having parties, enjoying themselves. Listening to Alton Ellis, now I know who the artist is, brings back such warmth, comfort and feelings of 'it's alright now', as it triggers those feelings along with the smell of jerk pork. As a Seven Day Adventist household it was 'forbidden fruit', but that scent was so inviting I could almost taste it and repent later! Now, when I go back one of the first places I visit is 'Pork Pit' which serves up all sorts of jerk loveliness, including pork. Mmmm...

You too, can pull out your memory capsule at any time.

* * * * * *

Chapter 6
The SPIRIT – Building Spiritual Life Muscles

Building physical body muscles is outside work, building spiritual muscles is inside work. It is a way to connect to the power within, the peace within, to live a life of purpose and fulfilment. All of us have all we need already inside of us. We do not need to look outside ourselves. When we enter within, we allow the energy to flow through us, bringing in feelings of love, peace and joy along with positive thoughts.

Life is never just a straight line, we will all have mountain top experiences, when everything is going so well and we are enjoying life to the full. We will also have valley experiences, when challenges appear, trauma happens or we start feeling like we are in a dark and lonely place. Building spiritual muscles helps us not to spiral into despair or remain in places of fear or guilt which prevent us from living our lives to its fullest.

Why build spiritual muscles?

It can help us to:

- Get through the hardships of life
- Build moral courage and confidence to move in the chosen direction at that time
- Diminish fear and give us a sense of empowerment
- Receive insight and the feel of the Divine
- Allow time to listen to our inner voice to make better informed decisions
- Remain centred and balanced

- Increase inner peace and wisdom to forge good habits
- Tap into gratefulness, happiness and joy
- Allow feelings of love to see the good in ourselves and others
- Work on our weaknesses while we acknowledge our strengths
- Stay within our higher self and take the higher ground in situations
- Build faith in our ability to stand strong in adversity
- Trust that the universe has our back.

Disciplines in building spiritual muscles

These could include:

- Meditation (or medi-pray as we say: a mix of meditation and prayer)
- Prayer
- Fasting: dedicated time out for spiritual matters not necessarily linked to a religion but a way of living
- Simplicity practise (think Ben Fogel and living in the wild)
- Solitude to help with self examination
- Silence – those 16 minutes pause a day to recalibrate and reorganise thoughts
- Gratitude and celebration time
- Journaling thoughts and feelings
- Being amongst like-minded people and loving family and friends. This opens the heart to experience good vibes and fresh love thoughts
- Being amidst nature – simple earth pleasures and using our senses to take in the sights and sounds

- Reducing distractions in order to give the mind a rest.

It is that 'contemplating my navel' time which allows for self-reflection, drawing on peace and love. Building our own rituals, traditions and practices can help to deepen our own spiritual practice.

When in self-reflection, we could ask ourselves questions such as:

- How am I feeling?
- How do I feel about X…?
- How do I feel about that person?
- Do I feel resentful? Like a victim or martyr? Or like a saint?
- Am I feeling sadness?
- Am I being judgemental or unforgiving?

It is a time to Stop. Breathe. Reset. It is a time to examine our fallback position to see if or where we may need to reset.

Within these reflections we create time to heal. We have the time to build on ourselves, rather than allowing reactionary fallback positions to dominate our lives, unless they are wonderful fallback positions of course! We have a chance to welcome in feelings of happiness, joy, peace, laughter and creating beautiful energy, rather than letting bitterness, moaning and resentment fester. We have the opportunity to change the whole atmosphere of a space for the better.

Many religions talk about 'arresting every thought', which

is similar to what we are saying. It is about being aware of our thoughts so we can choose whether or not we take the higher road at key moments in our lives.

Belief mechanisms

We all have varying lifestyles, systems, rituals, traditions, maybe even words and gestures we say amongst our family. Maybe we look to our ancestors for our roots spiritually, which could be American Indian, Aboriginal, Yoruba, Santoria or Candomble. Or maybe we look to our family faith; Hindu, Judaism, Christianity, Buddhism, Taoism, Islam, Sikhism, Shinto, Catholicism and many others.

Practices could include prayer, chanting, drumming, songs and stories, or it could be the way we set objects in the house or at an altar. We perform many rituals, whether we acknowledge it or not, at special events such as births, deaths, feasts, birthdays, holidays, seasons of the land, the passing down of heirlooms and the coming of age.

Our own rituals also come down to things we do every day, such as brushing our teeth or having breakfast a certain time every day. These rituals can root and ground us, get us through hardships in life and allow us to receive insight and feel the Divine amidst the mundaneness of our lives.

Let us look at our own life and decide which rituals, faith or beliefs we would like to practise to help to keep us rooted.

INSIGHT

The 'Slow Magic' of One Energy – Devon

As a physical therapist, I was aware that we used passive energy when seeing clients, through our touch. I was encouraged to do a Reiki course, to use energy in a conscious way. I signed onto a one-year Reiki course, which also happened to have shamanic healing, crystal healing, spiritual healing and regression within its modules. It was stimulating and exciting. I was torn between what I learned and the religion I had grown up in – Seven Day Adventist and later Baptist / Pentecostal. It took me down a route of thinking and seeking until I discovered my own path and belief that there is only One Energy, used in Reiki, mind work, spiritual healing and in fact any religion.

I better understood the different types of clients I treated, where some were not just looking for physical treatments but were also 'seekers'. They had a great sense of something more powerful, stronger and bigger than oneself, but not enough confidence or knowledge to put their finger on it. Thus, the MindBody Therapy business started doing Reiki sessions many years ago to talk, share and discuss spiritual and life matters as well as do a Reiki share. This also led to an understanding I use in my treatments, thus creating MindBody Tuning®, a combination of talk, mind and bodywork, and also the creation of One Energy systems of Healing®.

* * * * * *

ONE ENERGY Systems of Healing® and manifestation

When thinking about spirituality, consider One Energy, which taps into the universal life force, the energy that passes through every living thing on this earth and beyond. This energy taps into our conscious and subconscious, and we can use it to heal or to harm.

Energy is carried through prayer, love and all manner of thoughts and wishes. When you send love and healing to someone, that is the pathway it takes. This is the same energy used in church, for asking for forgiveness, for healing, for our purpose in life.

This is the most powerful energy around us but can we see it? No. Can we quantify it? Yes. From the time we ask for something in our thoughts, the Universe contrives to make it happen, the cogs start to turn and eventually our wishes will come true, but we must be patient and be aware of the words we use. If we sit still and dig into our pure soul, it will ask for what it needs, at its core being care and love for you and for others. It may manifest in varying ways, so staying 'open' to all possibilities and putting in the phrase 'or something better' at the end, will keep us 'in the flow' of the best version of our lives.

Use positive language, as the Universe has no sense of humour; it doesn't know the difference between what we say we want and what we focus on that we don't want. So let's be mindful of the thoughts and words, e.g. if you need a new job, it is probably best not to start with 'I hate this job, I hate getting up for it'. Start from 'I want a job to feel good, to look forward to every morning'. Using 'hate'

re-emphasises the word and the feeling, whereas we are trying to acknowledge it but also shift forward by leaning on the positive. In Chapter 8 there are useful stories about asking and manifesting.
So, let us lead with the positive, so we do not confuse our pathway, which is constantly being programmed by our subconscious mind, our nature and our fallback position about life.

Systems of healing

We put this under the banner of Reiki but many call it 'hands on healing'. Like a prayer for healing oneself or someone else, using 'One Energy' (people use their own faiths to do the same thing, thus we use the term 'One Energy' as a catch all). Focusing on the positive to reinforce it, we can place hands on ourselves:

'I am healing myself'
'I am making it better'.

If we are sending healing to someone not in our presence, use thoughts and words such as:

'Mum I hope you feel better and able to move around freely'.
'Grandad get better and be able to stay independent and stable in the mind'.

We may think they are normal words said in the mind, not even as a prayer or intent for healing, however they can be even more powerful if used with intent, belief and energy.

Thoughts are powerful; 'I am, I can', can impact our whole life and those around us because we are focusing on the positive. It is not to say we are in those thoughts all the time, but certainly aim for the majority of the time. By having belief that our words are powerful and these words are going out into the ether, we can start using words as mantras, which are words, sayings or sounds repeated regularly. We can do this in our 16-minute pause to help reset ourselves, to remove doubt, fear, guilt and bring in love, hope, faith and peace.

Take a breather

Sit or lie down now and refocus your mind. We will be training and building muscle to take our mind and body into total relaxation, to help with spiritual discipline. Read through first before following the exercise.

Close your eyes…

Take a long slow breath in for six counts and out for six counts.
Repeat until you can allow your mind to be still

Breathe in allowing the shoulders to drop… breathe out all you don't want in your body, mind, soul and spirit

Take a long calming, peaceful breath in and focus on your mantra, in your own words, e.g.
'I am powerful'
'I am…'

'I have...'
Breathe out, letting go of everything you don't want, e.g. anxiety, worry or pain

Repeat until you feel it and you are still in mind and body.

Visualise all the things, people and attributes you want in life, the positive things you want to bring into your life, your family, your circle, your home, your job, your space... imagine being in that life... feel it.

Believe you are in that space. Feel being in that space... who is around you? What can you see? What can you hear? What can you smell? What do you feel?

Seal it all by saying 'I believe'.

Stay there and allow your mind and body to be peaceful, gentle, at ease, at one with yourself and universal energy.

There is no time limit to staying here; be here for as long as you need, knowing you can come back here at any time, as you allow your mind and body to rest.

When you are ready, you can come back to your space, your body. You may feel like you've had hours of sleep but in reality, it could be that 16-minute pause.

When you open your eyes, come back to this space and allow yourself to feel comfortable, satisfied, connected, contented, peaceful, tranquil and calm.

When the universe presents our life to us, sitting in these moments, we have a chance of saying 'YES'. We can take action in our mind, if we accept any guidance being given. It could mean extra studying, loving a job or leaving a job, falling in love with your partner again or moving to another part of the world. It could be a pathway which takes some years to manifest, however start to talk it, visualise it, accept its offering, say thank you and step into it, even if that simply but powerfully means a new way of thinking and being.

I found this poem Wayne Dyer's book:
'There is a spiritual solution to every problem'
People are often unreasonable, illogical and self-centred;
Forgive them anyway.
If you are kind, people may accuse you of selfish,
ulterior motives;
Be kind anyway.
If you are successful, you will win some false friends
and some true enemies;
Succeed anyway.
If you are honest and frank, people may cheat you;
Be honest and frank anyway.
What you spend years building, someone [or something]
may destroy overnight;
Build anyway.
If you find serenity and happiness, they may be jealous;
Be happy anyway.
The good you do today, people will forget tomorrow;
Do good anyway.
Give the world the best you have and it may never be
enough;

Give your best anyway.
You see, in the final analysis, it is all between you and Above
It was never between you and them anyway.
By Dr.Kent.M.Keith

PART THREE
Building Emotional Stamina

This is the ability to stay strong under duress. We've all heard how great it is to think positively, but it is not the only way to build life muscles. There is a deeper work that can be done to discover how we are as a person, what makes us tick and what our 'fall back' position is. When building life muscles, we learn what is 'small' stuff, not worth fussing over and what is really important, so that we can let go, forgive and move forward in the best way possible. We can then start to believe in ourselves and in our ability to handle life's challenges.

Chapter 7
The SOUL – Building Emotional Life Muscles

Who would you say is managing their grief better? Someone who is wailing, or someone who is being stoic?

The answer is no one and both! We all come from different cultures and express ourselves in different ways.

Building emotional muscles means gaining the ability to deal with challenges and setbacks but also being able to bounce back mentally. Our emotions can cover a whole pendulum of feelings, all in a matter of minutes. We can respond in an open, even vulnerable way in the face of an intense emotional experience, where we are too upset to even move into being able to function… that is okay. We are present in that moment.

Emotions mean we are human, whether they are seen and expressed or not. It is how we are made, our response to life. Emotions are not 'good' or 'bad', they just are. We do ourselves a huge injustice by categorising emotions, but it is something we are used to doing, e.g. 'Don't be angry' or 'I shouldn't be feeling this way'.

Emotions are okay and help us to understand ourselves and situations, make decisions, and often play a large part in our behaviours, actions and interactions with others. What might be considered good or bad however, is the reaction or behaviour that comes from those emotions. Whilst the emotion might be out of our control, how they impact us, how we react to them, and how we in turn behave, is in our control.

We need to build emotional muscles to help us to:

- Be less discouraged over setbacks and look for solutions
- Regulate our emotions: pull them out or rein them in
- Be more adaptable to change
- See the larger picture to keep it all in perspective
- Recover quickly when we receive emotional wounds from words or situations
- Be able to bounce back from failure or rejection
- Feel less stressed: the ability to bring our stress levels down
- Begin to see the beauty within it all
- Begin to realise the lessons
- Be grateful and patient
- Bring forth calm, hope, faith and forgiveness
- Bring in humour and laughter
- Bring in confidence and tenaciousness for life again.

In life there are many times when it feels like the rug is being pulled from under our feet, without warning. One day we were carrying all the balls and suddenly, those balls go up in the air and never land back down in the same way. Life is changed forever, not necessarily in a bad way, just different. Sometimes sayings like 'when one door closes, another opens', can ring true at times like this. We know what is good for us at these emotional times, to help us to feel a little bit better but it is not always easy to do them as our minds are taken up with the pressing emotions.

Some ways to find relief during emotional times are to:

- Walk out in nature; touch nature; put hands in the

dirt and grow something, tend to something, see the seasons change before your very eyes and know that it won't always be this way

- [ ] Start a new hobby or anything that occupies you and your hands
- [ ] Invest more time with your family and friends
- [ ] Do some meditation and mindfulness
- [ ] Go dancing! Add in any other physical and/or fun activity
- [ ] Exercise, sleep well and eat well (after eating and drinking whatever you want at the height of emotional stress, calm back down to a maintainable healthier lifestyle)
- [ ] Explore your creative side with painting, drawing, pottery
- [ ] Go somewhere you have never been before to stimulate dulled senses
- [ ] Sit in silence, in nature and contemplate your navel (space to just BE)
- [ ] Give back to your community by volunteering or helping someone else in need
- [ ] Write it all down in a journal to help express your emotions
- [ ] Talk with someone.

Heartache and loss

According to John Bowlby, a psychologist, psychiatrist and psychoanalyst, there are four stages of grief and we all go through the same patterns when dealing with any kind of loss.

Shock and numbness

This is the phase where there is a sense the loss is not real and seems impossible to accept. There is physical distress during this phase, which can result in somatic symptoms: where a person has a significant focus, thoughts or feelings on physical symptoms such as aches and pains, panic attacks, stomach ache, chest pains and insomnia. If we do not progress through this phase we will struggle to accept and understand our emotions and communicate them. We will emotionally shut down and not progress through the phases of grief.

Yearning and searching

In this phase we are acutely aware of the void left in our life from the loss. The future we imagined is no longer a possibility. We search for the comfort we used to have from the person we have lost and we try to fill the void of their absence. We may appear preoccupied with the person. We continue identifying with the person (or thing) we have lost, looking for constant reminders and ways to be close to them. If we cannot progress through this phase, Bowlby believes we will spend our life trying to fill the void of the loss and remain preoccupied with the person (or thing) we have lost.

Despair and disorganisation

In this phase we have accepted that everything has changed and will not go back to the way it was or the way we imagined. There is a hopelessness and despair that comes with this, as well as anger and questioning. Life feels as though it will never improve or make sense again without the presence of the person we lost. We may withdraw from others. If we do not progress through this phase we may continue to be consumed by anger and depression. Also our attitude toward life may remain negative, full of regrets, hopeless and past oriented.

Reorganisation and recovery

In this phase our faith in life begins to be restored. We establish new goals and patterns of day-to-day life. Slowly we start to rebuild and we come to realise that our life can still be positive, even after the loss. Our trust is slowly restored and we may begin to trust that the Universe has our back. In this phase our grief does not go away nor is it fully resolved, but the loss recedes and shifts to a hidden section of the brain, where it continues to influence us but is not at the forefront of our mind.

We can bear these phases in mind as we go through different types of loss in the next section. Hopefully it reminds us that we are not alone. Our emotions are not unusual and we are not going mad or the only one experiencing loss.

Passing of a loved one

Inextricably, indescribably and understandably numbing, this section is about 'your death': not actually you but someone close to you, whose death you are experiencing. In the beginning, shocking, numbing, then acute, sharp, so painful, like an arrow in your heart, you wonder how you can go on. You wonder why people are acting normal when your 'love' is gone and how come the world hasn't stopped turning, when yours has.

There are no words.

INSIGHT

Finding comfort in the midst of grief – Karen

My dad just kept saying 'at such a time' when Mum passed away suddenly one Boxing Day, meaning that it was such a significant, forever unforgettable moment in time. Though he had his faith 'a friend in Jesus' to keep him company, as well as friends and his 'plantation' garden, loneliness kicked in for him. Of course he has us, his daughters, but we were not there when he had to go home to the 'dark house' as he called it. He could always cook and fend for himself like a good Jamaican man, so the only thing my lil' sis had to take over was the paperwork (especially once the bank told him to do his savings account on the internet…inter… what?!) as Mum used to do the paperwork. Eventually, he learned to smile and laugh again. Despite our own grief, being there for Dad gave us a chance to 'get to know' him more. (He said 'Mum had you all, she was your favourite', meaning that we always used to hang around Mum rather than Dad, she was our hub). This was our opportunity to make the best from something that was such a great loss to us all.

* * * * * *

It can take even longer, if the death is not a 'natural' one and the circumstances involve the police and a long drawn out trial and funeral. Then the aftermath of battling with forgiveness and letting go, which is on another scale altogether.

There are still no words.

It doesn't stop the feelings, but sometimes having something to focus on does help, that's why we all go back to work, the kids go back to school and eventually life moves on. How we move on depends on us, and how much we allow the feelings to flow through our body. Feelings of denial and anger, the what if, if only and dark depression… until the acceptance shift happens and each breath is a little easier, the heart not so crushed together. Sigh. Give it time, time that is relative to you, as everyone in the family will move on in different ways at different times. We cannot rush or slow down their journey.

So, it takes as long as it takes.

Break up – loss of a relationship

No wonder we feel so terrible after a break up, especially if we are the one who has been rejected or left behind. It makes it worse when you see the meaning of the word; unwanted, dismissed, inadequate, unacceptable or faulty.

Of course, words do not define us but the feelings can be overwhelming and emotionally unsettling; the pain and sadness, confusion, disorientation, anger, wanting to retaliate, anxiety, depression and jealousy.

What do you do with your life now, when all you have known is living and being with this other person, lives intricately woven together, only for it to be forced to unravel in a disorderly and uncontrollable fashion? You may feel like you cannot go on, however you DO have more inner strength than you ever thought you had and you WILL make it through.

You won't always feel this way. Time is a healer.

Ways to carry on:

- Learn whatever it is you are supposed to learn. Sometimes you can only do this by those sitting, glaring at the water kind of times (no matter how many parties you go to, you will inevitably have to sit with yourself again soon). In those moments when you go on those long lonely walks and try to figure it all out, though nothing makes sense, you are at least giving your brain, body and emotions a chance to catch up and come to terms with it all
- Write a letter to the ex – but burn it after you write it. Don't send it please! Ok go on if you must… see more in the 'letting go' paragraph
- Be kind to yourself and find a hobby to absorb you or a project to volunteer with, so you can help somebody else and keep busy
- Avoid rebounds!
- Keep the physical separation to avoid 'make up to break up sex' or the confusion of 'what did that smile mean? Do they want me again?' At least until some time has passed and you fall in love with yourself again
- Rebuild your social life, you are still you and have much to offer
- Counselling: if you feel like you keep making the

same mistakes or unhealthy choices, maybe this will help you to unpick what is going on
- Join a support group, even if they are your bunch of friends. Often you may find that your group of friends change, as they are all going through different stages, so you may naturally develop some new friendships with people who get it or are going through a break up at the same time as you.

We can end up bitter for the rest of our lives or we can choose to be happy and love ourselves enough to want to try love again. It can be a wonderfully cathartic experience: a cleansing or purging, providing psychological release through the open expression of strong emotions. Thus leading to new feelings, new experiences and new beginnings, now that anything is possible again.

Loss of Youth

Karen's thoughts, as a woman…
We were once a baby,
We were once a little girl,
We were once a teenager,
We were once a young woman with childbearing hips and perky breasts,
We were once a woman in the prime of her confidence, power and career,
We were once a woman with strong hair,
We were… once,
A woman.

What are we talking about? It is not so much the loss of womanhood but the time, typically in our 50s, when a sharp realisation occurs that we are no longer in 'that' prime of our lives.

This is not just about the loss of certain womb functions, but in general terms, the change that happens when we move from periods to no periods, from being able to conceive to very difficult to conceive, then suddenly we tend to notice babies, pregnant women, young seemingly vibrant women who could still have babies, who are in the prime of their lives and we start feeling aged!

We now know that me-no-pause, i.e. 'I don't want to pause thank you very much', can happen over a period of ten years or more, involving the perimenopause, actual and post menopause, as our body takes its time to mark the end of our reproductive years.

We are not the same as we were 10 or 20 years ago, so we start looking in the mirror and wondering where our youth has gone. We may not be 'ourselves' and we start looking towards retirement, yet we know we may have another 15+ years to work so what does that mean? We have to keep going.

One way menopausal women were described by Sigmund Freud is, 'Quarrelsome, vexatious and overbearing', pronounces Darcey Steinke in her memoir, Flash Count Diary: Menopause and the Vindication of Natural Life. No wonder they called it the men-o-pause; time for a pause on men as well as something they want to stay away from anyway! We need a better word.

Steinke suffered nearly two awful years of hot flushes, acute episodes that were like 'four-minute surprise anxiety attacks'. She sensed mortality stalking her. 'For the first time, I feel I have a time stamp, an expiration date.' She writes vividly and a little wistfully about sex, mourning her lost desirability, as she sees it, and the waning of her own desire. She feels angry; she yells at her husband. 'Early times of sexual frenzy seem almost impossible now.' As an author and educator, she describes this period so well.

How weird that this all happens just as we have usually come to the most confident and accomplished time in our lives. Then in varying degrees, with varying stories, we can turn from:

- Confident to always undecided: going back and forth in thought
- Uncertain of anything and anxious about nothing
- Feeling powerful and strong to more aches and pain in the body
- Saunter and swagger to careful steps, hot sweats, or dripping while we are in a meeting, on the bus or in front of an audience! These flushes are no respecter of person or place
- Full force ahead as Directors, Managers, Leaders, Nans, the heart of the family, to raging, low mood, anxious or depressed
- Being focused and on point, to inability to concentrate and do the same work which before took no time at all.

We can't give this full justice here, as there are many symptoms, however there are many books, podcasts, groups and remedies now out there, where women are freely talking about it, so we mustn't feel that we are alone. We can realise that this is yet another season in our lives where we will need big girl pants to navigate our way through without alienating everyone in our household! It is for us to be aware of what is affecting our day-to-day lives and be gentle with ourselves, seek the help we need and talk about it.

Darcy Steinke has also written about how she identifies with one of the few other species that enjoy a long postmenopausal life: killer whales. In the ocean, non-reproductive females play an important role. With the wisdom of years, they guide their pod to the best salmon. When kayaking in waters off the coast of Seattle, Steinke, hoping to commune with the whales, was rewarded with a magnificent breaching (a life affirming leap out of the water). 'The wild matriarchs have given me hope,' she writes. 'They are neither frail nor apprehensive, but in every way leaders of their communities.'

It is a matter of acceptance. Accepting our age. Accepting that our children, nieces and nephews are becoming adults, accepting if you are a grandma or grandad. Then switching to accepting the blessings it brings: whether wisdom, experience, knowledge of how to do life better, what to do, what not to do, who to be with, who not to be around, seeing how our lives have made an impact and to start looking at legacy and what it will leave behind.

We can then take on new roles such as keepers and carers, whether of our grandchildren or parents. We become the words of wisdom and the fountain of all knowledge, where kids and/or colleagues come to us for help and direction.

Instead of a shutting down, it is an opening up, a new phase in our lives, thus acknowledging that although one season of our lives is done, it is not all over. Our work is not done until it is done. We are still valid. We still have work to do and we are still relevant.

It can also be a lonely time for those of us in this stage, as we acknowledge that the 'kids' have their own lives and no longer need us like they used to. We have been through the mill, the wars, the nappies or navigating our careers and/or travelling. We've been through all the teenage angst, the exploratory 20s, the crowning 30s, the powerful 40s and now around fabulous 50, we should have a-mazing muscles to help us through the next 40 years of our lives! It is just a bit different.

All women will go through this, so maybe we can try to prepare the next generation to be able to handle and manage it even better, to talk about it, to get their GPs on board, and get complementary medicines ready for when they come to this season in their lives. Let us talk about it and share our stories. Let us come away from the shame and embarrassment and instead support and uplift each other.

Devon's thoughts, as a man…

We were once powerful: defender, provider, hunter-gatherer, family creator and guardian. To then be forced to take a step back to allow the young to come forth, even tearing down your ideas and challenging your authority, can be a tough experience as you get older.

To feel that what was once powerful, strong and revered by you is now literally drooping and even dripping, to be frank is like the dethroning of a king! Yet you have to smile and take your place further down the queue, safe in the knowledge that you have the wisdom, that you hold certain keys and tools of life.

Drowning, not literally, your sorrows, because you know what awaits the young bucks; but you also know that, flicking the page, you no longer have to 'kill and carry' the dinner. You now have others to do that, so it is okay to rest somewhat and reap the benefits of hard work, no longer tilling the soil but enjoying the fruits of your labour.

We can take comfort that we are, hopefully, becoming the wise one and that our power is now in the knowledge we have, the life muscles, rather than in our powerful physical muscles as we enter into a new era. We can use the tools we have gained in an acceptance of being in the now.

Women may go through the menopause but men go through man-on-pause; it is a pause on running fast for that bus, on chasing, on flexing physical muscles as life has thrown this curve ball. You may see it coming, but it still doesn't feel good at the time. If we look at our father or grandfather, maybe we get a foresight into what our life will be like as we mature. How does it look? How did they cope? Maybe draw on your perception of how it looks and if it is a 'grumpy old man' scenario, how can it be changed?

It is okay to feel aches and pains, let it be okay. It is okay to look at the female figure and do nothing, as you've been there in your earlier years, chasing. Immerse yourself in activities such as sports, gardening, family, reading and resting, all those things you never had time for in your peak years. Pause and give your wife/ partner the compliments that she chased for all those years, but you were too busy!

Allow yourself to take a different seat at the table and never give up on life, as you have many stories to share and life muscle lessons to impart.

Loss of Job

When we lose a job through redundancy, retirement (or even having a pregnant / baby break), we can be left with a loss of:

- A sense of purpose
- Of self with a title
- Self esteem
- Security
- Certainty.

We could start questioning who we are or how others see us without this job, this title, or maybe even dreading the question, 'So what do you do?'

It was especially tough during the pandemic from 2020, where many people not only lost their jobs, but the whole range of jobs that were available then, or would be available in the future, changed too. Whole industries were turned on their heads, forcing many of us to rethink how we work, where we work, if we still have to work and 'what the hell am I going to do now?'

This kind of loss can impact the whole family and lifestyle:

- Financially
- Emotionally
- Mentally
- Change in relationships dynamic
- Loss of daily routine, staying in more, changing the home dynamics
- Loss of colleagues, friends at work, whole social life gone (if we relied on it).

A whole stream of thoughts and feelings could start swirling around in our head and our heart, such as:

- How will I feed the family?
- How will I pay my bills?
- Feeling overwhelmed and alone
- What you feel you can and can't do anymore as family fun and holidays
- Angry at the one being let go
- Frustrated at not being able to do anything about it
- Feeling of betrayal from colleagues: 'Do I stay in touch?'
- Feeling of shame and embarrassment
- Wanting to blame someone for being in this situation
- Confidence wearing thin (especially as you apply for jobs with no response).

It could be time to:
STOP

- Keep it in perspective
- Look at the great and good things that have happened in your life

- Toughen up: life can be hard and you are not the only one who is going through this
- Start creating what you CAN be in control of
- Search out new opportunities for jobs, learning, skills or new hobbies; maybe you want to work part time so you have more time for family
- Assess your whole life to see what you really want to do from here and what you may still need to earn.

BREATHE… just pause… and breathe in deeply, dig deep so you can gather inner strength.

RESET and think about what you CAN do, what you DO have control over and what you CAN start now.

At these times we all know that we will have to bounce back, as we cannot stay in the doldrums forever. It is time to be honest with all our feelings, be honest with our family and ask for help where we need it most.

Loss of Personal Power

Personal Power is a mastery over ourselves, not others. It is being self aware enough to want to maintain a healthy love and understanding of who we are and the fact that we are of value. It is based on inner strength, confidence and a knowing that we are in charge of our thoughts, emotions and actions. This could show up in any area of life, such as our relationships, health, work or finances.
When we allow someone or something to take over that power, we lose all sense of control and responsibility and can easily fall into a spiral of self loathing and self destruction. The load then becomes heavy when we take

on other people's baggage, as ours alone is enough to deal with.

We could also recognise that WE may be the ones coercing: using power over someone, manipulating, dramatising and eliciting fear, anger or guilt responses in those we say we love. This is not love.

If this resonates with you, recognise first where you are with it or where you have been, then you can make a choice about it. Of course this is easier said than done, as it can take years to recover from power being taken from you, or to come out of the clutches of the benefits you may feel when you take away someone else's power.

Some ways to deal with this is to:

- Take back control and responsibility over your own emotions
- Let others do the same over their own emotions
- Put healthier boundaries in place
- Decide what is okay for you and what is not okay
- Change your language from victim to victor (solution focused)
- Instead of complaining decide to do something about it to regain your power
- Choose to forgive, let go and move on
- Realise the inner strength you had all along, you just needed to tap into it.

Loss in Retirement

Retiring is another big life event, which hopefully happens to most of us, if we reach beyond our 60s to 70s or even

80's. As we lose our daily routines, colleagues and full or part time income, it can seem daunting to face, especially if you live alone.

We may also realise that how strong we were as a young buck is nowhere near how we feel now, in the older version, especially after an illness or health issue, which often happens around this time. We may start taking more medicine and life seems to want to slow us down, whether we have done enough pension planning or not.

Stages of Retirement in general:

- First Stage: Pre-Retirement. The stage before you actually retire involves imagining your new life and planning for it
- Second Stage: Full Retirement
- Third Stage: Disenchantment
- Fourth Stage: Reorientation
- Fifth Stage: Reconciliation and Stability.

We suddenly have all the hours under the sun, exactly what we've been waiting for all these years. 'What if I could just get up and do whatever I want?' Well now it's here. Wonderful!

Then, after around six to twelve weeks of bliss and wonderment, we cannot believe we are saying, 'What do I do now for the next thirty years?'

Retirement is a new phase of life, so maybe it is time for different life muscles? Physically, maybe it is time for body strength training to add strength to the bones and a steady balance to our feet.

It could be where we look into creating new:

- Daily routines
- Hobbies
- Exercise regime or sports
- Friends
- House / home
- Grand parenting duties
- Volunteering interests
- Businesses
- Jobs – part-time
- Attitudes.

Although we may have anxieties around this time in life, it can also be the best time of our lives. It is still about our attitude to life.

However, why are we waiting until we are 'closer to death' for us to realise we should have been having so much fun before that?

Of course earlier life comes with its own strains of working, juggling, bills etc., but we still have a choice over how we deal with it all. Work, bills and things to get done will always be there, no matter how quick we are to get through our to do list. That's why we go on holidays, to get away from it all. However, what if, during each day we could also 'get away from it all'?

Take a breather
Stop. Breathe. Reset.

If you are not quite there yet, think about how to plan for it better. If you are there, think about how you can enjoy it more.

Some suggestions to help prepare:

- ☐ Save more money into your pension pot or other earnings pot
- ☐ Practise living on less from now on
- ☐ Make any financial moves, such as loans for loft building or garden changes while you are still in work
- ☐ Move to the area you want to before you completely retire so you can enjoy it and build up a network of friends and family support
- ☐ Rekindle your love with your partner by spending specific time with them on 'date nights' and see what hobbies or fun things you can do together
- ☐ Discuss together with your partner or children what retirement could look like.

Friendship loss

Different seasons of life mean that at some point we say 'hello' to friendships, and at other points we also say 'goodbye' to friendships. Building this flexible life muscle can teach us how to move on, let go, forgive and build even better friendships.

Great friendship attributes include:

- Quality over quantity
- Care over catastrophe
- Trust
- Respect
- Loyalty
- Empathy
- Listening ear.

Going through the pandemic could have totally changed our views about how important some friendships were to us at the time. Some were incredibly important and helped us through traumatic times, while others were not needed at all, at least not on a regular basis.

It is okay to say goodbye to friendships, as some will last forever and others will naturally phase out through the seasons of our lives. It can be heart breaking to lose a friendship, especially with someone who has been through some meaningful, difficult and heart warming times with us; someone who had our back, who knew all our secrets, guilty pleasures and memories.

Seasons of friendships:

- Childhood and school friends: with school friends, strong bonds are created as we go through first break ups, period pains, testosterone, the first drinks and parties, into college and/or first jobs. We are learning how to fend for ourselves. We lean on each other so much more than leaning on our parents or guardians. Friends know us inside out, through the lows and the highs, and we thought they would be with us forever.

- Late teens and early 20s: friendships are everything and everything is so dramatic: 'he said, she said', exacerbated by social media. In our late 20s we get to understand ourselves more, and what and who really matters to our lives. Thus, naturally friendships will change, as we realise we are all going off in different directions and maybe different parts of the world.
- Late 20s: it may be that we start moving around people who have children, as we would also like to settle down or at least have children. It could be we hang out with people who are focused on their careers, party life or hobbies because we have these things in common. Some friendships that we had from childhood may start slipping away as we realise that we no longer have anything in common. It is okay to draw a line under earlier friendships and maybe only meet up for reunions. People change, we change. It is natural to part ways, even if for a season.
- 30s/40s: children, school circles, family and friend units get closer due to the support that may be garnered from each other.
- 50s plus: we realise how much we can do by ourselves, as usually by this time we have learned to use our life muscles, so may not need as many friends as before. Though life could have thrown us many challenges, we have built up a trusted set of friends: some we grew up with, others we worked with and others we randomly picked up and stuck with!

Maintaining long term friendships

Many long term friendships go through all sorts of seasons and it is okay to say goodbye to that season and remain friends. It can be confusing and weird for a while, but if both parties respect and honour each other and still want to be in each other's' lives, both need to learn to move on and build that part of their life so another form of friendship can emerge.

We all change throughout our lives and not even friendship relationships can expect to stay static, so we can learn to grow with them as they teach us about ourselves. In times when we may want to cling on, we can trust to let go and allow the other person to do what they have to do and be who they have to be until they come back around. In times when we are the ones pushing away, we should try to do it with love, expressing how we feel and if we need space, understanding or just acceptance of where we are at in that moment.

There is no one size fits all as we are all so different, and different friendships can bring out varying magical parts of ourselves. We have to be honest with ourselves, and others, about what we do or don't need, and be brave enough to keep going with friendships or allow them to fade away, while appreciating what was.

At a time when there is so much uncertainty in the world, along with loneliness, maybe we can renew our friendships and learn how to reinvest in them to help enrich each other's lives.

INSIGHT

When you change but others don't – Devon

I used to be an HGV truck driver in my 20s and 30s, needing to work to live and make a start in life. I worked early mornings and late nights, so I was lucky to be able to start attending night school two days a week in London. When I embarked on a change of direction into health and wellbeing, it impacted me and the people around me. Some couldn't see me as anything but a truck driver and wanted me to live the same life. Others seemed to be offended. 'Who does he think he is, he thinks he's a doctor', said in a diminutive way. I stopped going into certain circles but also feel that certain friends and family alienated themselves from me, as they no longer understood who I was becoming.

My learning and knowledge changed their perception of me, but instead of getting to know this facet of me, they stepped away, as I think they may have recognised their own shortfall or desire to start something but never did. I later found out that even my bosses didn't have full confidence in me and were waiting for me to fail and fall back in line, to continue to be a good worker.

That first loss of some friendships was sad for me. It happened slowly over a period of time but when I looked at it, I also gained new friends, new goals and was too busy creating a new pathway for my life to really absorb the loss. Twenty years later, I can recognise some people who haven't changed, so we can no longer move in the same circles or live in the same 'village'. A nod, smile, quick chat at weddings and funerals is all that is left, with a tinge of sadness; but a whole raft of life muscles is the trade off, so there are no regrets as I accept and enjoy where I am at now.

* * * * * *

Teachment©

Some friends become needy in various phases of life, but of course if they have constantly pulled back your hair while you were sick in the loo or similar scenarios, then by all means be there for them.

However, there comes a point when we realise that some friends constantly just TAKE from us, rather than taking and giving, and/or they become toxic to us and where we are going in life. We then need to decide, are we benefitting by being a 'saviour' to them or are we supposed to move on to build healthier relationships.

Friendships can continue in a locked pattern of one being the drama queen and the other being the listener or loyal subject, until it just becomes exhausting to keep going this way. When one or the other changes, it also changes the dynamics, as maybe one of us no longer wants to 'be there' all the time to hear the same dramatic tales and gossip. When we stop showing up, the other person may act out because that is not what they signed up for, albeit at your expense.

If it gets toxic and full of 'he said… she said', it may be

time to have a word and draw a line. We may come across them at the workplace where it is hard to escape or we may marry into a family of them, but we can learn how to put boundaries in place so they are not taking us a for a ride we never paid for.

Feelings may get hurt on all sides but better the 'tearing' of the muscle in order to build better and stronger muscles, meaning that you will have learned how to navigate friendships and spot a taker (or liar, double crosser, excessive drama queen who drops emotional bombs, cheater, narcissist or whatever else fits the bill), as soon as you see one and use your muscles to put them right where they need to go. Then move on, if not physically, then emotionally and mentally.

Summary of loss

Sh*t happens! It is inevitable. The most we can do is try to live in the NOW. To accept what was and what is. To be fully present in the now with a sense of acceptance, accepting loss with eventual openness and love, means we can also learn (just about), to surrender to the unexpected, to let go our need to control and be brave enough to live and love fully, without the anxiety of 'what if'. That way we don't lose out on our own precious hours of fully living and fully being present.

Forgiveness

What is forgiveness?

It is the conscious choice to release feelings and thoughts of pent up anger, resentment and vengeance against yourself or someone else, whether they deserve it or not.

It is not always easy and it can be hard to see how a difficult and challenging experience is supposed to help us heal, learn and grow but remember, we have more strength than we ever imagine and can dig deep to forgive.

Forgiveness is for us, not for them. It doesn't mean we forget what they have done to us but it does mean we don't allow them to have a level of control and power over how we love and live the rest of our lives.

Forgiveness looks at how we think and feel about ourselves and others. It helps us to look at our thoughts and feelings and how that relates to the energy we allow to stay in and around us. When we feel... if we pause long enough to experience the feeling... then look behind it, there is often a thought, which could be a fleeting one or come from our belief system, which drives that feeling, which gives it energy. That energy can often get trapped in our bodies, until it also becomes a physical issue. Often we know where in our body hurts or get uncomfortable when we think about a certain person or situation, thus the mind/body connection.

If our thoughts are, 'I will never forgive X or I can't wait to get back at X or I cannot forgive myself for doing X' then we need to see how this is affecting our lives and the lives of those around us.

For example, if a Mum never forgives her ex partner for cheating on her and chooses to withhold the children from seeing not only their Dad but also his parents, that action has a knock on effect. Of course we could say it's their fault, but our constant reaction is our choice.

When it is the pain from a heartbreak situation, we are upset, hurt and disappointed. However, let us not allow it to eat us up, as it can fester in us and poison us, rather than them. We can move on. Say goodbye. We can wish them all the best in life (that bit might take a while to say or even think!).

Ultimately, time is the biggest healer.

When we forgive, the life muscles getting used include:

- Taking back our personal power
- Taking charge of ourselves and our emotions (goes back to being able to regulate ourselves and staying self aware)
- Clearing the wounds from the past, from our heart and mind
- Growth and new ways of thinking about our past, present and future
- Building strength and endurance for other changes in life
- A release of thoughts spinning out of control
- Understanding ourselves and others better
- Healing from the original experience.

It does take time and sometimes there are many layers of forgiveness, like an onion, that we may have to work through. For some, we may forgive and that's it, we've moved on. For others it may take many sessions of talking, writing in our journals, meditation or talks with those involved before we feel we can forgive them and move on.

Yes, it is okay to talk to the person concerned where possible, if you feel you are ready. Sometimes, the person may not even remember it as you do and may not even realise the hurt they caused. Often you may not get the reactions you would like but it will help you to get it off your chest and off your mind, body and experience. If it is not possible to speak to the person, speak to them in the ethereal or write them a letter you never send.

Take a breather

Are you ready to bring forgiveness into your life?

Find a piece of parchment (holy) paper (or plain paper will do) and write down and finish these sentences. It doesn't matter how long it takes, whatever is supposed to come up and whatever you are ready for will come up.

I now forgive myself for...
I now forgive X for...
This is what I want to say to X... write the letter you won't send.

Letting go

Letting go in this instance is freeing ourselves from something or someone who no longer serves us. That doesn't mean just walking away if we are in committed positions, relationships or jobs; it could also be a matter of freeing our mind rather than extracting our physical being.

Imagine that we have our life in a suitcase and we have to carry it around with us everywhere we go. Then our friend has enough of carrying theirs and we say 'yes' to carry it for them. Then a member of our family dumps theirs on us and we go into work and someone else is having a bad day and they dump their bags on us as well.

Can you see how burdened we can be, just on a daily basis, if we do not learn how to say 'No' or simply put stuff down, tell people where to pick it up and walk on.

Life muscles getting used include:

- Knowing the best use of our energy and time, so we don't become or stay exhausted
- When to be kind to ourselves and not allow toxicity in our life
- Learning not to carry to carry other people's stuff, along with our own
- Acknowledging how we feel and knowing when to Stop… Breathe… Reset
- Acceptance of what is, in the now
- Empowering ourselves to live our best life and move on from the past
- Feeling the fear but pushing through anyway

- The realisation that we cannot make someone love us or do what they do not want to do
- Bringing in support mechanisms for ourselves.

Again, letting go does not mean that we forget what the person has done or even what we have done. However it does mean that we do not allow another moment to be wasted thinking about what was done or not done, said or not said… and let go.

Take a breather

The pieces of parchment (holy) paper from the forgiveness exercise can be used as a method to release and let go another layer of all the hurt and pain you may have felt. Normal paper can also be used.

Spiritual ritual to let go:

Write on the parchment paper all you wish to release and let go of. Use it to wipe down your body as a symbol of releasing and freeing yourself. Use your words and thoughts with the intention of feeling free as you burn the paper (in a safe space outside). Let go of someone, something or thought processes as you see the paper fade away, as you see it go up in smoke. Allow your body to feel free and say goodbye to habits, thoughts, fears and regrets and celebrate your freedom.

INSIGHT

Letting go when you can't do any more – Devon

It is a great joy to be a parent, allowing them to fly and be who they are, whether we like it or not. I have two sons; one is finding his way in the world, but the eldest has stumbled and fallen, though we have always tried to support him in finding a way to help himself. I always thought both parents need to be on board and on the same page when giving teachment© otherwise the child will find the route of least resistance, the weakest link and exploit that. He now lives life in a way that is not sustainable. How far do I push myself to keep helping to make his life better if he is not willing to participate and invest in his own life?

After 18 years of age, I had no more jurisdiction, no power, according to the state, so I've been watching him slowly committing to a slow death through addiction. I think he can see it but is not willing to build that life muscle, to make that final choice and of course chemicals have done their own work. I used to get involved and try to help him but it was like pouring water through a sieve, so I had to separate my ego from 'my son is so capable of being a footballer, a doctor, anything he wants to be' to the reality that I cannot bend his will to mine. I had to step away emotionally as it broke me, especially in being the bad guy all the time because I wanted him to stop. Also, I had to deal with the guilt, question of faith and self-hate feeling for a long time, the 'what did I do wrong?' until I asked him one time, 'Are you happy?' He said yes, so I stopped working so hard, like he knew something I didn't know.

It is extremely hard to let go of so much time and effort put in and it is painful to see him or talk about him. It is easier to help someone else's child than my own as there is way too much emotion tied into it and it's very sad. I'm still learning to 'let him go'. He knows I'm waiting for him to say 'I'm ready now' any time we speak, but I no longer need to feed him as he is not a child.

* * * * * *

Dealing with other strong emotions

There is absolutely nothing wrong with any emotion, it all comes down to how often we have which ones, how we deal with them and how that affects us and others around us.

Anger

Anger means a strong feeling of annoyance, displeasure or hostility. Reasons for being angry can vary from feeling hurt, used, taken for granted, taken advantage of, embarrassed, lied about, attacked or shamed, all the way up to full on traumatic life experiences which have changed the shape of your world.

Anger is not just expressed in an explosive way, which is easy to recognise. It can also be repressed and come through as being:

- Mentally exhausted
- Overly sarcastic
- Overly critical
- Mean and/or non-emotional

- ☐ Sad
- ☐ Depressed
- ☐ Using diversion to avoid facing emotion
- ☐ Physically tense thus experiencing more aches and pains.

So, what do YOU do when you feel that strong wave of emotion come over you?

Do you vent, scream and shout it out or do you count to ten and calm down before expressing how you feel?

It's likely that we've all vented at some stage! However, if it becomes addictive, maybe we need to ask ourselves why?

Is it because it feels good in the moment or is it the reaction we are after?

If it is the reaction, why are we looking for that? Do we feel like we are not otherwise heard or taken seriously? What is the thought trigger behind that fallback position?

Can we, over time, reset ourselves as necessary?

Take a breather

Run through those questions again and examine a time in your life when you consistently felt angry about something or someone, or just vented for no good reason.

It helps to write it down, especially if you do it in a timeline, so you can see what else was going on in your life at the time. This could highlight stress factors and give you further understanding about yourself.

INSIGHT

Pillow release – Karen

We were always taught that there was nothing wrong with being angry, it's how you expressed it or dealt with it that counted, e.g. did we let it fester into revenge, hatefulness, take over our whole lives, stay resentful? I remember my anger as a child, especially after being told off or told to go upstairs away from the TV so my Dad could watch the evening news on the one black and white telly in the house. I would express my indignation by stamping my feet noisily up the stairs, only to be told to come down again by Dad, to go back up respectfully and quietly. So I reverted to screaming into the pillow instead, which he couldn't hear! I still keep a pillow for moments like this, which can be therapeutic in helping to let go of angst and anger.

* * * * * *

Ways to manage consistent anger in the moment:

This does not stop us feeling the feelings and sometimes for good reason, however it gives us tools to build life muscles to help us to cope with the feelings.

- Stop sit still in those feelings and allow them to wash through you until your body comes out of panic or fight mode
- Breathe take a long deep breath in, while you raise your arms and let it all go by breathing out and swooshing your arms down at the same time

- Reset especially if being angry no longer serves you or you know it feels good but you are being prompted to let it go
- Count to ten before you speak or express it!
- Go back to the Take a breather… earlier to delve into what triggered it
- Go for a run or walk
- Talk to a loved one
- Put on some music to dance and change your own energy
- Write it all out in a journal or draw it out with artistic expression
- Do a good deed for someone else to take your mind off your own battles
- If at work, go to the toilet to calm down first
- When you are ready to express yourself start with 'I feel…' rather than use accusatory tones and language
- Reach out for help from your GP, a counsellor, a CBT practitioner or other trained person if you are ready to delve deeper into any issues.

Ways to manage being on the receiving end of anger:

- If you believe it is not about you, do not take up their baggage
- Put a bubble around you (imagine a superpower cloak or good spiritual energy), even temporarily, to protect yourself from their words, actions or intentional silence
- Protect yourself from their rancid energy (another word for rancid is 'bad mind'), especially if they are being mean and malicious

- Use scents, sprays or incense as a ritual to help cleanse yourself and the space
- Wait for them to calm down before asking what is wrong
- Give them a Healing Hug until they are ready to talk about it
- Continue to show them love even if you get nothing in return
- Top up your own pot by speaking to family and friends, not necessarily about the person
- Cover them and the space with peace, joy and love, by your intent, so you release any mounting tension
- Put yourself in their shoes, see and feel what they are not saying verbally to see if you can help
- Reach out for help for them or yourself by finding a counsellor.

Disappointment

When we expect something or someone to be or do something, we can get upset, sad and feel at a loss when it doesn't happen. Instead reality happens, which ends up being nothing like we imagined. Enter disappointment.

It is even worse if we are coming from broken places, where the people who are supposed to be there for us have let us down time and time again, causing a breakdown in our ability to trust.

Disappointment comes with an emotion of deep sadness, laced with anger, resentment and emotional anguish, and it is really uncomfortable. We may feel like we want to lash out at the person who has let us down, and sometimes there is a time and place for that.

However it is up to us how much we let it take over our lives.

Where thought spirals of disappointment can take us:

- We compare our life with others. With social media, it is so easy to get snippets of other people's lives and compare ours with theirs.
- We hang around negative thinkers. Our environment shapes us into the person we are. If we hang around people who support us, encourage us and lift us, our life will move in positive directions. If we hang around negative thinkers who encourage our constant moaning over disappointments, they can suck the life out of us. If you find that the majority of your friends bring you down, consider exploring new social circles.
- We may be in a career we hate. We spend over 40 hours a week investing in our careers (more often than not, it's closer to 50+ hours). That is a huge amount of our daily lives. If these hours are spent investing in careers that we despise, we will more than likely become disappointed and unhappy. If we find ourselves in this situation, it may be time to consider other options. Try researching new career options, building a project on the side or getting career counselling.
- We may get into substance abuse and /or mental health issues.

INSIGHT

The disappointment of feeling abandoned – Devon

Not knowing my parents until I was ten years old, coming to England from Jamaica, I already knew disappointment. I grew up with it, always wishing and hoping for my parents and feeling not wanted. It's a familiar Jamaican story for many 'left behind' children from the Windrush generation. I grew up with my grandparents who had no time or energy for a little boy. They had strict religious Seven Day Adventist rules and no warmth. I had no pictures of my parents, no imaging, no value creation by walking in my Dad's shoes or seeing my Mum to bond with her. It left a deep disappointment I tried not to repeat with my children by being present in their lives.

It hurts and is hidden under other guises, hardly talked about, without the knowledge and understanding of how it has been affecting us, emotionally, mentally and physically. It was important for me to have a knowledge and understanding of life muscles as it helped me to reflect on the sense of abandonment. Being afraid to have or love too much as someone might leave – how would I give my own children that imaging, to close that void from where it should have come from?

I'm still learning and grateful I can step back and stand in stillness and thankfulness that I can do a lot for myself, to go forward and create a better next generation. I have a responsibility that I need to use to not repeat the past to my children, nieces, nephews and so on. I believe in karma and may not see all in my lifetime, but I will try and pave the way for them, then it will be up to them and their life muscles to do the same for their children. I've learned, as I've gotten older that life is not as serious or dramatic as it appears to be in the first instance and that anyone in any situation can Stop... Breathe... Reset. To slow down, step back, not to react too quickly but see a bigger picture and put energy out there positively.

* * * * * *

Frustration of life not going your way

If you are pushing against a wall, sometimes it is hard to smash it down as it is not for you right now. Next time you could put one finger against the wall and it comes down, or even better, there is no wall! We all experience this at some point in our lives, when life is just not going our way.

We may just want to run and scream and have a big 'ole tantrum like a two year old! We may think it feels like the end of the world, when sometimes there is nothing we can do, except move onto Plan B or C.

Are we even going the right way?

There is a time to row against the tide when forging ahead with goals and you know you just need to reach the ocean, then you will be flowing with the tide. But when is it time to stop rowing against the flow of the tide, and start allowing the boat to float with the current? Are we supposed to stop resisting and submit to the flow? Could it be that we are going on a pathway that is not meant for us?

What are the signs saying to you? Is there an inner knowing that really, you are not supposed to be doing this, or is your Spirit saying that you are in the right place, it's just a bit hard right now?

No one to blame

Sometimes, when stuff happens, there is no one to blame, it is no one's fault. We may have mad conversations with ourselves, sometimes with no answers. We may blame God or the Universe for not showing up when it was needed, for not saving that person close to us. All valid human thoughts as there really could be someone to blame.

Though we may take it too far when we blame someone else for being broke when we spent more money than we were supposed to. Or when we stayed in a job we hated because we didn't have the guts to retrain for a better job, and so it goes on.
There are things in our control and some things out of our control. We need to take responsibility for 'our" stuff and leave the Universe with the rest. That is ok.

Maybe the clarity on the 'why?' plus the 'oomph' to do anything about it, evades us today.

Stop. Breathe. Reset.

We cannot always work it all out in one day. Tomorrow is a new day, with new possibilities.

Take a breather

- Make a list of the expectations that are causing your frustration (just a short list, no more than 5 items).
- Make a list of new, adjusted expectations that make it easier to accept the situation that frustrated your old expectations.

Teachment©

We pray or wish for a new house but wood keeps turning up, we pray for a new job but courses keep showing up, we ask for fish to feed our family but a fishing rod keeps showing up. Do we get the metaphors?

Sometimes, the thing we need is staring us right in the face, we just had such a fixed picture of how it should turn up that we are blinded to the opportunity given to us.

Betrayal

At times like this we can be left feeling angry, flummoxed, overwhelmed, shocked, ashamed, helpless, thinking that the wool may have been pulled over our eyes, vulnerable, powerless, guilty, or dealing with lies and wondering if we had anything to do with it.

A friend, a partner, a lover, a parent, a work colleague, whoever it is that has betrayed us; it hurts a lot. It is even worse when it's from someone you didn't expect it from, like ever. Trust is broken and that damaged relationship will never be the same again. Even though it can be healed, it will be forever different.

When we have let someone into the inner sanctums of our hearts and minds, it can be worse because when we hurt, we start to clam up. We close our heart to protect ourselves, we start cowering in the shadow and love is shrouded over.

Should we forgive them? Yes. Go back to the forgiveness section, it always affects us more than it affects them.

Should we continue a relationship with them? It depends on how severe the betrayal and how often, and also is it real, imagined or 'small tings'. For example, they left the toilet seat up or down again, when you already had a full blown discussion about it and agreed to leave it up or down, and now you feel betrayed. Just saying that betrayed is a strong word to use in this instance! Maybe you are feeling upset or disappointed even, but again over 'small tings'.

This is in comparison to someone using all the money from your joint bank account without telling you, or telling all your family about something private between you or having an affair with someone. These are bigger issues.

Go back to the previous paragraphs about letting go, disappointments and especially anger, to explore ways to manage.

Fear

Sometimes we reach a barrier and think we can never get over it because we allow fear to take hold. Yet instead of fear, what about reaching into our spiritual selves rather than thinking that our physical self has all the answers. See how to delve in further in the Building Spiritual life muscles section.

Fear is like a brake. It can stop us in our tracks. On its own, it's not a bad thing, as it is warning us there is danger ahead. If we want to overcome the excess fear, we have to push past it and through it.

F.E.A.R.: False Expectations Appearing Real

We must try not to allow it to overcome us; we can stay alert to it but still live fully. Some ways to help include to:

- Remove ourselves from the daily noise of all media and social media discussions, and filter what we allow ourselves to watch or listen to
- Have conversations about it
- Reach out to our family and friends
- Use our hands to occupy ourselves, e.g. bake a cake, swap recipes, plant food in the garden, plant pots on the window or balcony
- Rebuild broken relationships
- Let sunlight in, to combat fearful thoughts
- Have fun, play music, play games whenever possible to balance out rising fear
- Walking for 30mins for five days a week will help with stress, circulation, mental health, muscles and bones – just being in nature is sometimes enough.

As we say to our clients, 'what is the worst thing that can happen?' Now imagine that, find solutions or acceptance of it all and put fear down.

Fear can stop us acting on the nudges life gives us, telling us to go in a certain direction, to study a new thing, to jump into something new.

So, remember to keep it all in perspective as our own barriers may be real or imagined.

Take a breather

Stop. Breathe. Reset.
Go back to the chapter on how to make the Building Life Muscles program work for you.

When you go through the steps, you will discover that you have the power and ability to change your inner state. Our inner state determines how we filter, and then interpret, our inner and outer perceptions in order to create the stories we live by. The way we respond to our stories creates our emotional life, thus allowing fear to creep in.
When we reset and are feeling good and energised, it is easier to create encouraging stories that enable us to act with patience and courage towards events, towards other people, and towards ourselves.

Let us be brave and do a bit of what we love because the world needs what we have. We can step out and make a difference in our part of the world. We can't all be Rashford or Michelle Obama ('damn!') but in our own way we can give, love, share and be kind, wherever and however we can.

Being happy and content

Happy feelings are fleeting and can change at the flip of a conversation. True happiness doesn't rest on what is happening externally, it comes from our choice of what we believe within. If we try to rely on others for our happiness all the time, we are setting ourselves up for disappointment. We upset our own self from time to time, so we are bound to upset others and cause them to feel unhappy at some point.

If this happens to us, it is our choice to stay there and spend the whole day in that 'funk'. However to choose to stay there after time has passed, is also up to us. We can create our own happiness by doing the things we love, which make us smile and make us happy.

We need to practise loving ourselves, and staying in love with the life we have chosen.

INSIGHT

Knowing your happy places – Karen

One of my 'happy' places is within music, whether that is by myself or with friends at a festival. Other places are releasing tension through exercise, especially walking through nature, and topping up my family pot with love and laughter. That one lasts for ages, where I'm full of love and open to say 'yes' to life, to the Universe and all is well again.

* * * * * *

So why do we sometimes find it hard to admit when we are happy? When everything is going our way, when we have received what we have asked for, we are looking around our home, workplace, park or even holiday space and enjoying it, with the people we love, we can in that moment, admit happiness.

However, we are sometimes fearful of it, as if we expect bad things to happen next or something to interrupt our life. It is normal, especially when experiencing any traumatic events, to be tentative about really enjoying times of peace, love and happiness. However, we might as well really be present and enjoy it, as we are not always in control of what comes next. Our state of being doesn't stop the world turning, but it can affect us, and those around us on a daily basis if we do not allow happiness in.

Guilt is not a productive emotion, yet it is one that we feel a lot. We may feel it when we start to change our behaviour to allow for happiness and focus on ourselves. People who devote their energy to helping others often feel guilty when they work on their own happiness.
If you're someone who continually helps people, you might have difficulty letting go and working on your own journey to happiness. You don't have to feel bad because you are taking care of yourself; that is a good thing as it

means you get stronger before helping others again.

Pursuing happiness can be difficult when it stirs up unexpected feelings of guilt. We may feel guilty about being the newer, happier person we've always wanted to become. Being happy sometimes means breaking away from others who held us back, and it's normal to feel guilty that they are not able to find what you did at this moment in their lives. But remember that we don't have an obligation to make others happy. We can be a good friend, relative or partner, and be there for our loved ones and point them to help; however we cannot make someone else happy.

Working towards being happy can force us to face emotional pain. We may have wanted happiness so badly, and for so long, that it hurts. It forces us to visit things that were painful to us in the past. If we allow ourselves to feel beautiful feelings of happiness, love, gratitude and pleasure, we may also grieve the feelings of the loss of time and past feelings of sadness. We may have clung onto those feelings, but now the nudge is to let go and allow happy in. That is okay.

If social media affects your happiness

When we are overwhelmed with social media, it is time to step back and out of it. We can have a day off or incorporate sleep 'hygiene' where we switch off the phone at least an hour before bed, so we are not consumed by imagery which is not always real or connected to our lives. Before we know it, we are comparing ourselves to others, thus affecting our own self-esteem. We have become so dependent on social media for validation, as if a few comments or likes from some random person should make us happy.

Instead we can go back to forming real relationships, having face to face interactions where we can, so we 'feel' the person and listen to their whole being: e.g. not only what they are saying but how they are saying it, their body language, their eye movements etc. We can validate and ground ourselves with a real connection to ourselves and others, with real social interaction and the uplift that comes from that.

Stop. Breathe. Reset.

Know yourself first. Approve of yourself first. You are enough. Not because someone likes you or you have X followers; you don't have to wait for these to be your A-mazing self.

Sometimes we spend more time looking to see who's looking, before we just get on with what we need to get on with, the doing or the being. Does it really matter to your actual day-to day-life? What matters more, the perception of your life or the quality of your life and how it impacts others?

It may matter if we are influencers and it could affect our bottom line, but for most of us, it doesn't. No one has it altogether all of the time, no matter how great their social media looks, so switch off from social and on to your life.

When you are feeling happy, building life muscles and sowing seeds of inner strength:

- Practise gratitude
- Write down what you are thankful for every night
- Help others and sow seeds of love
- Write down what you love to do
- Write down 'I am happy now because…' and finish the sentences.

Remember, however, that having 'more' does not necessarily bring more happiness, so focus not on 'if only, or when X happens then I will be happy', but I am happy because…

It is best to write as much down as possible, as it is a great way to look back when you need to rely on those muscles later in life, when there may be a bigger, deeper reason not to be happy.

Take a breather

Rocking chair test
If you were 90 and in a rocking chair, what would you want to say about your life?

How closely does your life reflect your answers now? What would you say you wanted more of in your life? Are there small ways to action this in your daily life or to plan towards it?

Allow your happiness to shine through. Do the best you can, when you can, that is all you can ask

of yourself. Take off the big boots and stop kicking yourself, instead
You made it to here, despite all the ups and downs, the challenges that you have faced. You are still here.

Be the life you want now. Be still in that for a while.

Choose happy.

PART FOUR
Improve your Resilience

Chapter 8
BUILDING LIFE MUSCLES – Practical Use

Resilience is the ability to bounce back from disappointments, failures and pain, whether in the body or in life. It is the ability to recover quickly.

Staying the course with our intimate partner

Couples who are resilient feel good about their relationship because they have confidence that they can weather the storm through tough seasons within that relationship. They know that life never stays the same but when committed, any conflicts can bring them closer together and lead to a deeper understanding of one another.

In order to reach those moments, each person has to feel secure within themselves and able to trust their partner's core; that they are who they say they are, which is shown in their actions, reactions and by 'showing up' and being present in the relationship. Maybe there are two questions to ask here:

1: How secure are you within yourself?
2: How secure are you within your relationship?

It is not just about the other person but also what we are bringing to the relationship table. The relationship table is where we lay out everything that we bring to the union: not only tangible assets such as property and money, but also things we cannot buy such as life experiences and qualities including stamina, tenaciousness or flexibility. It is also about our personalities, such as gregariousness, creativity, assuredness or logical thinking, and also our core values: what matters most to us such as faithfulness, connectedness, honesty and integrity. These all add to the fabric of our intimate relationships and the foundation in which they grow.

Teachment©

Some people describe their partners as 'my better half'. For some this is said tongue in cheek, but for others this may very well be the case. What this may suggest, however, is that we are not already whole ourselves. We may then put too much pressure on our partner, if we expect them to do things for us to make us whole, happy or fulfilled, when that job belongs to us first. We need to take ownership of that, to make ourselves whole, happy and fulfilled. Of course we are never fully 'learned or perfect' and can always be challenged for further growth within ourselves, and the relationship, if we are open to it.

* * * * * *

Attachment Styles – how we relate to others

John Bowlby, a psychologist and psychiatrist, studied and developed the attachment theory for adults and came up with four attachment styles. He uses this theory to help us understand not only what we bring to the table, but also

where we may have started in our lives and how that may affect how we are in our intimate relationships.
Our attachment style may change over the years, and can be influenced by our partner's behaviour during this time. Major life experiences can also have an impact on how we evolve, which in turn can affect how we are within our relationships. Thus, it is important to build our own life muscles, because we are not just responsible to ourselves. Who we are and how we behave also has a cause and effect on our partner's life, any children and any blended or extended family unit involved.

Our style is about how we perceive and deal with closeness and emotional intimacy; our ability to communicate and listen to emotions and needs, our expectations of our partner and our methods of responding to conflict.

Couples who feel comfortable with each other tend to:

- Feel safe when the other is nearby and responsive
- Share discoveries with each other about themselves
- Engage in close, intimate contact with each other's bodies
- Feel secure, even when the other person is not available, either physically away or mentally busy e.g. studying.

The four attachment styles are:

1. Secure / Connected
1. Dismissive / Avoidant
1. Preoccupied / Anxious / Clingy
1. Fearful / Disorganised / Avoidant

Secure / Connected

Comfortable with oneself: able to be both intimate and independent. Easy to get close to our partner and low on anxiety and avoidance.

Dismissive / Avoidant

This type is Independent, self-sufficient and not looking for a partner's availability. Uncomfortable with closeness and avoids vulnerability from themselves and their partners. Finds it difficult to trust and depend on others and prefers not to depend on anyone, thus remaining rather distant.

Preoccupied / Anxious / Clingy

High on anxiety, wants to be close, clingy and feels insecure when the other person is unavailable. Worries that their partner doesn't want to be close or doesn't love them as much or will abandon them. Always seeking approval and prone to being manipulative.

Fearful / Disorganised / Avoidant

Does want closeness but fears that it may hurt them, yet at the same time needy for intimacy. Can be negative and have trouble trusting, as well as finding it hard to manage emotions.

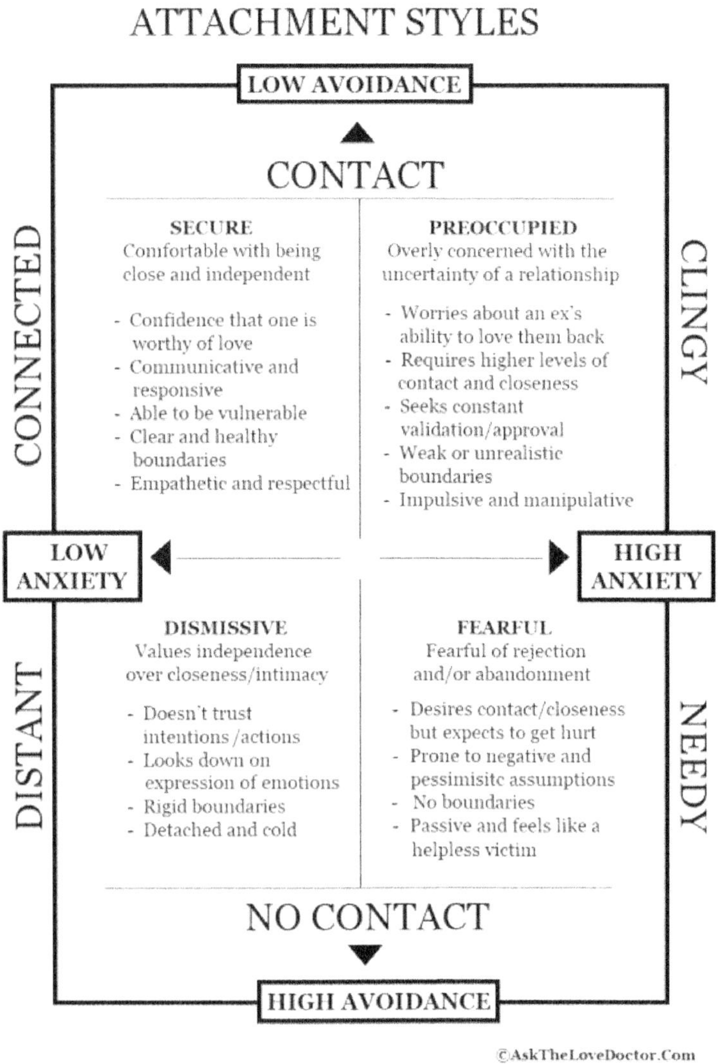
ATTACHMENT STYLES
LOW AVOIDANCE
CONTACT
SECURE
Comfortable with being close and independent
- Confidence that one is worthy of love
- Communicative and responsive
- Able to be vulnerable
- Clear and healthy boundaries
- Empathetic and respectful
PREOCCUPIED
Overly concerned with the uncertainty of a relationship
- Worries about an ex's ability to love them back
- Requires higher levels of contact and closeness
- Seeks constant validation/approval
- Weak or unrealistic boundaries
- Impulsive and manipulative
CONNECTED
CLINGY
LOW ANXIETY
HIGH ANXIETY
DISMISSIVE
Values independence over closeness/intimacy
- Doesn't trust intentions /actions
- Looks down on expression of emotions
- Rigid boundaries
- Detached and cold
FEARFUL
Fearful of rejection and/or abandonment
- Desires contact/closeness but expects to get hurt
- Prone to negative and pessimisitc assumptions
- No boundaries
- Passive and feels like a helpless victim
DISTANT
NEEDY
NO CONTACT
HIGH AVOIDANCE
©AskTheLoveDoctor.Com

These are four extremes. We may find ourselves, or our partner on a sliding scale of intensity within these styles. We may fall in and out of the categories as we go through life's challenges, or we may recognise ourselves in more than one style. Below is a picture table of the four attachment styles.

Wherever we find ourselves in the attachment grid, let's stay aware of what is going on with us and our partners, so we can work on being the best partner we can be, bringing the best out of ourselves and our partners for a mutually beneficial and healthy relationship.

Where we are doesn't have to be where we will stay, as each season of life can make us feel stronger or more vulnerable at any time. However, if we are flexible, adaptable and have a partner who is also willing to be aware and work on themselves, we can choose to align ourselves to create our own relationship rhythm; thus creating an interesting tapestry for our lives, evolving into what works best for both of us, in a healthy and giving environment.

The treasure of relationships

Most of us want to be with someone, so when we are in a relationship, we sometimes need to remind ourselves to treasure it, to look after it, and almost see it as a separate entity: you, me and 'US'. We can then commit to looking after all parts of this trinity.

It is 'A-mazing' when everything is going well, we feel like we are on the same page and we are full of laughter and private jokes. These are great times to consciously increase those wonderful 'memory capsules', which we can pull on when storms start raging in life.

The best assumption is that love already lives here. Love then has to translate into other forms as we start building the relationship muscles of:

- Respect
- Communication – sharing stories and experiences
- Commitment to 'US' – strengthening our bond
- Connectedness – 'We're in this together'
- Patience and understanding
- Kindness and compassion
- Healing Hugs and kisses
- Fun and Lightness
- Having a project to do together
- Acceptance
- Compromise and sacrifice
- Forgiveness.

Just like any relationship, feelings sometimes run hot, sometimes lukewarm and other times cold. It is realising that and knowing that nothing stays the same, life is always changing, people are always changing, but that it is okay when it fluctuates. Feelings may flutter like the wind, but a choice to commit stays solid.

Whether married or not, when 'for better or for worse' kicks in, of course you do what you can, you step in and then you're like, 'shxx! Is this what commitment means?' Recovery from the challenges of life, such as illness, financial struggles, family traumas or dramas doesn't happen overnight. You start building on or up different areas of your relationship, discovering different stories as you talk, building resilience along the way; hopefully strengthening the core foundation of your partnership, and knowing 'we're in this together'.

We cannot always see around the corner; we don't know what is coming but we must trust that we have the strength to get through it. We also know that although we are together as partners, we still really walk this path alone. We battle with our own fears and doubts, therefore managing ourselves first and foremost always remains paramount.

INSIGHT

When you go through rough stuff – Karen

When Devon was suddenly in pain in 2019 and had a hospital stay that culminated in major surgery seven days later, we were closer than ever as a couple. I knew he didn't want to rely on me. Plus, he's not really a touchy-feely person, not as much as my family anyway, but we must have held hands more over all those days in hospital and after, than in our entire time beforehand.

I also saw a softer side come out of him; tender moments shared. What did Devon need? I couldn't help him, but maybe the nurses could? Did he need water? When someone is ill and sitting still, like in hospital, or maybe when we are still, it's amazing what you can pick up from just the smallest nuance of facial expression. Those were scary moments, moments we had to face alone and in our own thoughts. They were also moments to treasure, something experienced together that we could look back on and say, 'remember when…'.

* * * * * *

Of course, in those quiet hours, we can feel very alone and may not be able to 'reach out'. That's when our partner needs to have our back, but it's also when we have to dig deep into our own reserves to remind ourselves, 'it's going to be okay, we've got this'.

It is also so important to keep our own support network close, to help us through rough times as we cannot always do it alone. Whether that be family, friends or church, when our backs are sometimes against each other, we will both need different people to lean on and talk to, especially when we are both hurting.

Communication

'The biggest communication problem is that we do not listen to understand. We listen to reply.'

Stephen R Covey – author of The 7 Habits of Highly Effective People.

INSIGHT

Men are from Mars... Karen

In general, women want to talk more than men, that's why it is so important to have our sister friends to have a good ole chinwag with, to get things off our chest. Women can look at, say, a pyramid and want to talk about its colour, stones, textures, where it came from, then go around the other side to see if it is looks different, then discuss that. Men, in general, see a pyramid, say it is a pyramid, walk around the other side and still say it is a pyramid at this height, width and depth, and the five-minute conversation is done.

If women revive the conversation again, men think we are repeating ourselves! However, we know that we are talking about something totally different about the pyramid that we hadn't looked at in that way before. Women want to be listened to and we are frustrated when we feel we are not. Some men may respond by feeling a need to retreat to their 'man cave' to be left alone, though this retreat could be right in front of us, in front of the TV.

* * * * * *

We suggest that couples have an hour a week, to provide a time and safe space to share anything, to talk about themselves or other issues in the household. Though even that may be too long for some!

'We have two ears and one mouth so that we can listen twice as much as we speak'. Attributed to Epictetus, a Greek philosopher.

When we listen, we can hear all of what the other person is trying to say, rather than be waiting for them to stop so we can say our piece. It is about reaching an understanding of the other person, as well as being able to articulate what we are really trying to say.

For example, our partner may feel that they are being moaned at when we ask them to take the bins out, when from our perspective, we just want help with household chores. So what is being said versus what is being heard? It would be healthy for these things to be discussed and agreed, rather than assumed. We can slip into these roles without thinking, but if one person is constantly doing it all it can build up resentment.

Maybe meet in the middle. Have a talk. Work it out. Do things to keep the household going, but also as small acts of kindness for each other, to meet the other person where they are at.

Author Gary Chapman has identified five Love Languages, which are:

1. Quality time together
2. Physical touch
3. Words of affirmation
4. Gifts / tokens of affection
5. Acts of service.

Do you recognise your own love language and that of your partner? How can we use this love language?

INSIGHT

Tea for Two

Devon
I always make two cups of tea or other beverages, when I'm making myself one. It could also be fruit or dinner but it shows respect and that 'I see you'.

Karen
This is Devon's love language, though I may prefer him to say something, as I like to hear things. So a love language may be how one person gives love, but may not be how the other person receives love. Again, it's about reaching an understanding of each other.

* * * * * *

Some people have certain behavioural patterns due to their nature and nurture. It is not possible to 'change' a person, they have to willingly want to or care to change or participate. It is also about us accepting that this is the way it will be and learning to adapt to that, as it doesn't mean the person loves you any less, they just show you in a different way than you expect or need.

If we never quite speak or understand each other's love language, or we remain out of sync for a long period of time, it isn't necessarily the death knell of the relationship, particularly if there are other ways in which you each show love and respect.

There are also ways we can give ourselves the love that we

need, in the way that we need it. We cannot expect our partners to provide every fix for us. We can supplement ourselves and maybe we can receive it from safe places such as our family and friends, and activities that make us happy. Some might seek that 'shiny' new thing, but healthy personal growth and development is deciding to commit to each other every day. If a 'shiny' new thing does come along, are we really ready to blow up our lives for it?

Small 'tings'

Have you heard the saying, 'Don't sweat the small stuff'? Well small 'tings' is similar. Say it to your partner often to remind them that a big blow up about 'who is cooking what tonight, you ate my last chocolate or you drove the wrong way', doesn't have to stay big, especially when it really doesn't matter. Someone has to drop the ego and the shoulders, admit it is 'small tings' and just let it go on behalf of 'US', and on the same day if possible! It is not always that easy, and it can cause issues if one person feels like they are backing down all the time. Sometimes we may need to review the whole picture before we fling words around like 'you always', and ask ourselves, is it actually true?

We all have moments or seasons when we go through trauma and loss, or have big events like anniversaries, births and weddings, which take over our lives for a while. There are also seasons of study and/or career advancement or having a baby, where one partner needs to lean heavily on the other, which is totally expected.

We may also have feelings of:

- Being constantly judged or judging
- Feeling drained
- Resentfulness
- Unreliability
- Lack of trust and jealousy
- Being constantly preoccupied and vacant.

This is where one partner may have to keep rowing the boat for a while, which is totally fine. However, to stay in these feelings consistently throughout the relationship is a different matter.

If we recognise that this has happened in yet another relationship, this is a red flag, and a time to dig deep to discover why these types of people keep getting attracted to us or vice versa. We are the common denominator in all the relationships we have. Is it always their fault?

Abuse or coercive control is a different topic altogether which we will not be going into here, but please get help or point someone to get help as soon as possible. It is never acceptable. See further help and references at the end of the book.

As we reflect on where we are at in our own relationship, the Seasons chapter also covers the many changes we go through in life, where we really do need to build our own life muscles to pull not only ourselves, but others through as well.

Where there is love, there is hope. We don't know what tomorrow brings; all we can do is choose what we do today. Choose commitment. Choose love.

INSIGHT

Choosing the moments – Karen

As I drew really deep breaths walking down the aisle by myself for the second time (they were really deep breaths as everyone keeps reminding me, they could all hear me! I didn't realise how nervous I was), the most I could promise my husband was:

'I will love you today, because today is all I know. I will love you today, because today is full of hope.'

I reckoned that if we both chose to love every day, we wouldn't be fixated on the 'what if', but enjoy being fixated on the moments.

* * * * * *

Teachment©

It is to remain open to love every day and not be closed. Love allows healing to take place when we are brave enough to be naked and vulnerable in front of another. Healing builds life muscles by allowing that part of us which no longer serves us to be shed, allowing a metamorphosis in our love lives to take place.

Family relationships

The quality of our lives depends on the quality of our relationships. Not everyone is blessed to have a strong family structure, however it can be created from the people we grow up with and other family and friends we meet along our life path.

Family bonds that are resilient usually have:

- Shared belief systems
- Good communication (though it is never all day, every day!)
- Common purpose
- Flexibility
- Adaptability
- Stability
- Supportive backbones
- The ability to rebound and bounce back from petty arguments or trauma.

We can help to build family life muscles by:

- Always celebrating the good stuff
- Pulling together for big life events whether they be weddings or funerals
- Encouraging each other
- Coming together consistently
- Supporting each other through life
- Praying together
- Playing together.

Different cultures may have certain rituals, celebrations, religious events and/or prayers that are built into their family structure. These too can help to maintain and grow the family bond.

INSIGHT

Memories of Purpose and Play – Karen

'Train up a child in the way it should go and they will not depart from it. Honour thy mother and thy father, so that you may live long. Children obey your parents in everything. The family which prays together, stays together'.

These were some of the sayings and scriptures I and my siblings were brought up with, coming from a Pentecostal background, though sometimes I saw them as propaganda when we were 'straying' away doing our own thing, and needed scolding to remind us to do what we were told! Nonetheless, it didn't hurt us and our parents covered it in love, unlike many church members we knew.

We had family prayer meetings, where we had to come with our head covered in a scarf or beret, and bring a song or scripture, at least two times a week. Most times we tried to keep it lively, with our family favourite chorus 'Praise Him, Praise Him, Praise Him in the morning, Praise Him in the evening'.

These were rituals, along with church all day every Sunday, but coming home at lunch to luscious rice 'n peas, curry goat, chicken, macaroni cheese, coleslaw and salad, made by Mummy's fair hands (started off before we went church in the morning, she was a busy lady).

This was offset by us seeing our 'jokey Daddy' (not the strict 'God' father), when we had enough money to go on caravan holidays with two other families for a week in the UK. We had such fun: cricket, rounders, football, skating, ice cream, chips and doughnuts! These were also our rituals, and it helped to build good family life muscles of play, fun, common purpose, faith, support, celebrations and pulling together. It gave us all great memories and good backbone.

* * * * * *

No matter how great or small our family is, or whether it has good stuff or not so good stuff, we can try not to take it for granted and to work on improving our relationships where possible. Of course, it is not always possible and sometimes acceptance of how someone is can be just as big as forgiveness. We cannot control how someone else is, we can only control ourselves, and what we do, say and think.

However, we shouldn't underestimate how much influence we can have over the other members of our family, especially any young ones, and how our behaviour can affect them. We've heard many stories of how one side of the family has been cut off because of what went on between partners, where there was no abuse but only scorn and a great deal of hurt, which can affect the children's outcome in a sometimes irretrievable way. It affects not only that immediate relationship, but also how the children may manage their relationships later on in their lives.

Do we really want to cut off grandma or grandad, aunty, uncle, sister, brother, cousin because of 'our beef', our issue? Of course, many issues are valid but do have a good look at it again, just in case there is a reconciliation available; if not with ourselves, then maybe with our children or children's children.

Other people's problems: perception, position, power and proof (O.P.P)

Some people in families can be very controlling and manipulative, which can exert influence on our lives. How much are we allowing them to dominate us, to have power over us, hurt and control us?

There comes a time in our adult life, where we have to take a stand and decide what we will allow in our lives and what we won't, and that includes family members. Sometimes, it is all about them and their problems, and there really is no need for us to take them or their issues on. We can listen but not absorb it into our life. We can try to accept them for who they are and where they are, without them being in our inner circle.

It doesn't have to be a complete cut off – just a healthy boundary – but it also doesn't need to affect how we are in the rest of our lives, including the other people we love. Maybe we can decide where they need to be in our circles of support and if it is way out there, for our safety and/or sanity or our children's sanity, then that is also okay.

If drama or destructive behaviour is happening in our lives, we might take on the emotional and mental challenge of getting any help we need. It may be us, bringing our problems, position and power into our family unit without realising the damage it is causing. Let us get help if we need it, to change our behaviour and pull together, rather than apart and help support our family unit. We can find ways to celebrate the small wins, even amongst 'we have no money' woes; if we get down to basics, love, games and laughter need no money. Remember, muscles have memory, so let us check our fallback position, reset it and start again. It is never too late to try and repair broken relationships and to build better family life muscles.

If you do want to shift, to move away from unwelcome thoughts, people, conditions and conversations, then move away physically if you can, or at least mentally. Some things that challenge us may be in our DNA or generational (family pathology) – which has nothing to do with us, yet we still have to deal with the remnants.

A family pathology of discord can have a profound affect on the emotional intelligence of the children in particular. If we are coming from places of discord, we are so busy dealing with trauma that our energy goes into survival mode, rather than into having aspirations, goals and ideals, which is how it should be. Other areas such as emotional and spiritual development fall by the wayside. Thus, everyone's 'success' is different and can be viewed from the place we start, rather than 'we or they should be here'. For example, getting up for a job every day may be one person's level of success, starting a business to sell at £1bn may be another person's level of success.

Dig deeper. If this wasn't handed to you from your

parents, get further support and back up, as we can learn to deal with that 'stuff" and let it go so it doesn't become a part of our experience, or for those who follow us. We can deal with it without blaming our parents, the past or the children. As an adult, we can decide the future, so we can learn to take the reins of responsibility and build those life muscles.

Take a breather
Stop. Breathe.

Pour two full glasses of water. Now pick up one glass, and hold it at arm's length with your arm straight out. Feels light and manageable doesn't it? Now imagine having to hold it in that same hand for 30 minutes. Notice how unmanageable and heavy it has become? Now pick up the other glass using the other hand and hold that at arm's length too. Think about what you are doing and why.

Holding other people's stuff is like holding the two glasses, learn to put them down!

Reset.

Teachment©

Carrying other people's baggage, our baggage, or the baggage of not forgiving or judging ourselves and others is very heavy. Can we be compassionate and kind enough to ourselves, and our families? To put it all down and allow the healing to take place?

We know how important it is to be the best version of ourselves as, even if we have no children, our nieces and nephews are watching us, are following our family patterns. So let's see if we can change the conversations, change the energy and atmosphere and create healthy roots to keep everyone grounded.

Parenting (role models)

Ideally, parents are responsible for helping the next generation build their life muscles, so they can learn to handle life at its highest, toughest level. Even if you are not a parent you are still a role model for someone.

Parents are the builders of generations. Will the offspring be prime minister, a criminal, a lawyer, maybe a speaker at the UN?

Who are we shaping?

It all starts from us.

If our upbringing was tough, will we swing the other way and not be so tough on our children?
If we had nothing, will we give our children everything they ask for?

We all need balance in our lives and nurturing children is no exception. To build life muscles, maybe they don't need to be coddled, pandered to or treated with kid gloves. Of course they need protection, of course they need to stay 'kids' for as long as possible, but they also need to experience life's responsibilities and consequences. Especially as children become teenagers and start to spread their own wings, give them more chores so they realise not only how their contribution matters, but that they need to contribute in the first place!

INSIGHT

The importance of discipline – Devon

When it came to boxing, the training was harder than the bouts, and it took discipline to get there. I had to get up early to train, when I was 13-15 years old. In general, I think we have taken away training and discipline from youngsters too much; especially from young people who do not fear anything, or respect the law or their teachers.

I believe that too many of the principles and structures of discipline were taken away from schools, and parents struggle to discipline when they should – choosing to be their children's friend instead of parents. We give children too much sugar and not enough salt; saying yes when we should be sticking to no. This is where if they are given too much candy as a child, they lose all respect for you as the soft parent since they are used to being said 'yes' to. It's like loving someone to death.

In my own personal experience, they may use light drugs such as marijuana and have been told it is nothing, until they then go onto hard drugs. I cannot express my full disappointment that people were still using kid gloves with this person in my life, even though they eventually became an adult and could make their own bad choices.

I feel like choices were taken away from the child, a choice that could have helped them build better life muscles. They now have no feet, no grounding and no backbone, as everything is being done for them… an addict in a 'nanny' state system. Everything is given to them without work, so they find it even harder to push themselves out of this situation. Since they now have 'milk and honey', why would they?

Everyone's story is different and as parents/role models, we can only try our best to give them all they need to be set up in life. Even if we give them the best, they still have the agency to act independently and make their own free choice.

*   *   *   *   *   *

Teachment©

It's important to give children salt every so often, so they get used to life's ups and downs and realise that life is not sugar all the time. Sometimes maybe they need to go hungry, see the fridge empty or go with you to the market and help carry the shopping bags (remember those of us who used to have to go to the market with Mum and pull the trolley, so embarrassing! Though you knew Mum worked hard and shopped hard, especially when she used her negotiating skills with the market stall holder).

This way it becomes part of the children's experience that food and money doesn't just magically appear in their life without them acknowledging and appreciating the work you have to do to get it there. They need to go out there get their part time job and experience making money, contributing to the household, buying the food and cooking it, so they understand the circle of life. Is it too late for the next generation, where food is delivered already made or cooked, directly to their doors? Time will tell.

Work

What has building life muscles got to do with work?

With the 2020 pandemic changing the way many of us work forever, there is much that we go through at work that affects our whole lives, especially if we are working from home as well. We can go through highs, lows, disappointments, rejection, bullying, criticism and the list goes on.

Whether we enjoy the work that we do or not so much, we may all have to do it at some stage in our lives. Whether we do it resentfully or joyfully is up to us.

Remember the fallback position versus how we can reset our thoughts, emotions and actions to respond differently? We can also do this when we need to when it comes to work. This builds life muscles such as:

- Flexibility, when the job or position changes
- Patience, when the colleague next to us or over the

Zoom meeting puts us down all the time or speaks over us

- Kindness, when someone is going through a hard time which affects their work
- Resilience and determination, when we are rejected for a promotion or a new position
- Confidence and assertiveness, to help promote ourselves
- Wisdom, to know when to speak up and when to keep quiet, while remaining a team player
- Managing our own stress levels while taking on new tasks or staff members, juggling our work and their outcomes, without taking it out on them
- Learning from mistakes when they occur
- To accept any sharp criticism, in order to move forward and be better informed
- Self-awareness – to know whether that irritating person is triggering something in us that needs our attention for growth.

There are many more life muscles that apply to our working lives, it is up to us to find out what skills we need and acquire them to advance our career, if that is what we want. Either way, we all have to deal with our own lives and work, colleagues and bosses at the same time, which can be taxing on both our mind and body.

When we are going through tough times we may feel like we hate the work we do, but we may not actually hate the work, it may be the people, the environment or the culture of the workplace. We have to ask ourselves, 'Why am I at work? Am I here for what I need in the future? Am I here to provide for my family? Am I here for my career or am I here because I'm too scared to move on?'

It is up to us to get our priorities in order, and know the best time to stay or move on, according to our personal circumstances.

Building relationship muscles in the workplace

At work, we can often be thrown together with people from all walks of life and if after the pandemic we aren't in the office as much, it may be a good idea to join a local choir or community group. This gives us another outlet, as well as feeling a sense of community.

Work, however, could be the only opportunity we have to talk to people outside our normal peer group, age, culture, race and lifestyle. This not only widens our breadth of knowledge about people, but also our tolerance of each other and the communities we live in. We need to learn to get along with people with kindness, and being at work is no exception.

Even without being in the office environment, there may still be people who will try to name and shame us via email, get one up on us and/or bully us. Or it may be the work culture that bullies us into submission, whether it is 'all work, no play' or 'work hard, drink harder'.

Working continuously into the night and weekend might be okay if we are working on projects with tight deadlines, but it is not sustainable in the long run and will lead to burnout. Yes, it is up to management to ensure their staff are not overworked without breaks, but it is also up to us to manage ourselves, to put lunch breaks in the diary, book our holidays and discuss priorities with our boss, so we know what is most important without working until 9pm every night. Sometimes, until we speak up, managers may not realise the strain they are putting on their teams and want the work done without thinking how it is affecting our personal life. We need to use modern tools to work smarter with increased productivity rather than harder.

It is up to us to put the boundaries in place, especially when dealing with bullies. Decide what we will allow and what we won't, and who we can speak to about it. We can also look at ourselves to see if there is a pattern of behaviour to allow 'them' to act this way, or indeed for us to act that way.

Take breather

What is our trigger point? Let's see if we can identify our fallback position and decide how we want to reset (ref part 1 chapter 2).

Trigger	Fall back – Automatic Thought	Reset – Replace with a new Thought or Positive Affirmation, Word or Action

Teachment©

If you are starting a new job you'll have to find out where are you fit in and have an understanding of how the land lies. You naturally need to check out the people, the culture and also figure out the real hierarchy, to see where you fit into the food chain. Then become aware of your own skills, how powerful you are and step by step to build up your own reputation over a period of time, without jumping in with both feet or trying to displace anybody. It is important to be able to take a stance, you will need to be able to hold your space and be able to take on whatever is in front of you, until such time that you recognise an opportunity for growth and/or career advancement.

If you are treading water and doing a job as a means to an end, know why you are doing it. In the meantime you can study, learn from those around you, plan ahead, take action and 'Power Up' your life when the time is right to move on, upwards or across. Or if you are staying, see how you can make it more interesting and fall in love with your work again.

'Do what you have to do, until you can do what you want to do' – Devon

There are more exercises, tools and tips in Karen's book 'Power Up for the Year'.

Diversity and Inclusion

In this section we will not be talking about all diversity

and inclusion, as that is a book in itself, but we will share our own experiences as black people living in a predominantly white society, where our experiences, our talent is not always recognised or our contributions are downplayed. We talk about it because this is a particular challenge that we have to teach our children about, in order for them to build life muscles to cope with what they might have to face when it comes to the race question.

INSIGHT

Coming to England - Devon

After arriving in Britain, via a ship, at ten years old, I still had no formal education, leaving school at 15 years old, but I've never been unemployed and always strived to get jobs as well as buy and sell items to make money. I moved schools so many times, from Nottingham to Birmingham to London in the 70s, I did not give anyone a chance to label me educationally subnormal (which was often the case for many black children and children of immigrants). Each school had a different curriculum but I covered my tracks well, even though I couldn't read or write properly (I now know that I had dyslexia). I learned to quickly adapt, fit in and speak 'the language' of wherever I found myself.

Coming from Jamaica, I was confronted with racism in England though I didn't understand why it would be so just because of the colour of my skin. However, I had other battles to fight as when I did meet my parents for the first time ever, I was called a 'dunce', or they thought I would ‘never succeed or hold down a job’. In Jamaica, I wasn’t educated so much at school but I was useful, as I was already ‘educated’ by working, selling fruit from the farm, calculating the money and using my common sense. In England, the perception was that because I had no English education, I was stupid.

Overhearing these comments started stirring something within me and made me determined, building the strength in my own mind, to prove them wrong and find a way to work. When finding manual work, the ‘n’ word was used a lot, or derogatory or coded comments were made but covered with ‘but not like you Dev, the others’. If I said anything they said, ‘you got a chip on your shoulders’. Then there were the skinheads to deal with on any night out, so we travelled in pairs or packs to avoid getting caught by them alone and possibly beaten up.

However, amidst all that, I was to find myself homeless after my Mum, and then Dad separately decided to go back to Jamaica without me, and I was kicked out by the landlord. Though I was taken in by a white family of one of my friends, it ‘blew my mind’ because they were a white family who didn’t see colour but saw me as a human being, so I soon left there as it didn’t match the concept of what white meant at the time.

I had to build life muscles to survive out there and although I got into fights, I knew I didn’t want to end up on the wrong side of the law, so it was either risk going to prison or work hard and keep my head down. I worked and learned to drive a HGV truck to earn more money.

My journey has helped me to realise that there is only one race, the human race. At work I was racially abused many times, but rather than allow it to beat me down, I used it to spur me on to work harder and earn more. There were good white people and there were bad ones, just like there are good black people and bad ones (plus complicated ones like my parents who didn't offer me any help). It helped me to see a balanced picture. I strived to do good and be good to all, rather than wasting my energies to keep fighting the ignorance on both sides.

Spiritually I knew karma would kick into my life, as 'what you sow is what you reap'. So, I couldn't physically keep whacking the guy who kept saying 'n' constantly in my face, I had to deduce that he had 'mental issues' at the time as my way to explain it, as years later he wanted to be my friend. I couldn't forget but it did serve me better to forgive.

As we can understand, dealing with family issues as well as racism brings its own challenges. For some black people over the years there has been a constant denial of self, especially for black men as they have always had to duck their head to not be perceived as a threat as they walk the street or enter a shop. It is like a denial of who they are and a reduction of themselves for others. It has been the same for some black women, especially in the corporate world, to lower their voices, change their accents and reduce their personality to 'fit in' and not be seen as an aggressive 'angry black woman'.

Of course, we all change a bit when we go into the varying arenas of our lives, such as work, play, family or sport, and people from other countries or regions may also feel the need to change their accent amongst certain people to not be seen as 'foreign'. We all make judgements about people: on their clothes, their hair, their walk and their demeanour. However, nothing can be done to hide the colour of someone's skin, when an immediate judgement is made on first impact.

There have been consistent reports over 40 years in Britain about institutionalised racism within government, sport, the Police, even the NHS. We talk about it as it is real, so let us continue to have conversations, to sit down together and broaden our understanding of why racial quotas and affirmative action were introduced. We are glad it is being addressed and displayed by some organisations and companies even more at this present moment, but we still have a way to go.

* * * * * *

Mental health and racism

There have been many studies linking racism, including micro aggressions, e.g. being treated differently for the colour of your skin, to issues with mental health. Categories of micro aggressions include those that appear as overt discrimination, prejudicial behaviour, abuse or harassment. In many cases, the aggression can be difficult to pinpoint and resolve because it is not so outright and obvious, or even malicious.

Apart from the normal 'we must please the boss' type mentality, black people often wonder why it is sometimes so hard to toe the line and to 'fit' in to what people refer to as the majority (in England being white). Even when we try to understand it, on many levels, it seems to be extra hard work for us and can cause an underlying dis-ease in the mind and body over the years.

This is what Yvonne Coghill CBE OBE, refers to when she researched this in her studies after years of working with the NHS - she writes about weathering: the premature ageing and sense of erosion due to constant stress, psychological and physiological. This is in regards to dealing with consistent prejudice and racism, thus the effect it has on our mental health and well being.

We find that mental health has a wide spectrum but can trigger:

- Anxiety
- Anger
- Frustration
- Emotional trauma and mental scarring
- Higher blood pressure
- Depression
- Chronic stress
- Substance abuse.

It can leave us feeling:

- Devolved as a human being
- Pigeonholed into certain professions and roles
- Marginalised
- Powerless
- Traumatised by injustice.

INSIGHT

My Dad's journey - Karen

Coming to England (after the 1948 Windrush ship), my Dad also came on a ship, in the 1950's, unlike 'posh' Mum who had an airplane ticket. He had sold a business in Jamaica so he and a best friend could get to England. He was an ambitious man who got vex (angry) at his first pay packet, since he expected to earn more in England. He eventually became a foreman in a factory. There was one white man who said things (micro aggressions) and threw things on the ground out of jealousy that a black man got the job, until Dad had to go to the manager. Although he didn't want the man to get sacked, he did want him to behave the way he did either. Dad didn't want to admit that racial abuse was also 'getting to him' (causing mental health issues), and didn't realise the extent until he started speaking to the manager and tears started edging out of his eyes. There were no more problems in that workplace.

In another work place, a racist, Dad's words, made up lies about him but in the end the man got sacked (karma?). When asked, how did he manage in a racially abusive country at that time, he says he prayed about it and got on with it (the silent weathering that was taking place) as he needed to provide for his family. His church was a safe haven but even there, people will be people, so he learned a long time ago to trust God, not people, but to love them, hate what they might do but to focus on how he lives his life, not on others.

* * * * * *

Despite the racial trauma passed down from generation to generation, second generation Caribbeans in the UK had parents who wanted us to do better than they did and, on the whole, they pushed us to get our education in their beloved 'mother' country so we could become teachers, social workers, accountants, lawyers, professors and MPs.

We now teach our third generation children all we know. This is the 'Black British' generation as many were born in the UK. They benefit from dual/blended cultures. Now propped up by improving recognition of the contribution of their forebears, they seamlessly traverse between cultures employing both their British and Caribbean heritages.

However, they may still feel the 'rage' of having to hold their tongue, dealing with both subversive and overt racism. We still have to teach them that wherever they go, they must build life muscles to:

- Push to get help, even if on the first attempt the GP or maternity nurse doesn't take us seriously and even if our own family say 'just get on with it' (although there is an element of 'getting on with it' as well)
- Talk about our feelings of marginalisation as we are not the only ones who have been through this, it can help to trigger hormones to calm our nervous system
- Focus on what you can control (the third generation will no longer stay for long where they are mistreated, unlike us in the second generation)
- Look for support within your community as there are Windrush and next generation who can share

stories of how they managed in their time

- Embrace yourself and your ethnicity and culture
- Read, educate yourself on all matters of discrimination if you need to identify it
- Get active – involve yourself in diversity and inclusion activities and speak up. Raise your vibrations
- Challenge the status quo e.g., decolonise curriculums of schools, colleges and universities
- Channel the 'rage', join groups, vote, be creative, bring humour, bring meaning and purpose to any movements, let it off in dance or church/ rituals (no wonder we used to clap our hands so ferociously and sing the chorus 20 times! It was a safe space to be amongst our own, to shout, express, sing, dance, be ourselves and to let off steam in the 60s and 70s in the UK, instead of fighting mods, skinheads and the NF (National Front)).
- Acknowledge small signs of hope and things which have already changed in the UK and help the continual change
- Stand on the shoulders of all those who have gone before us, who have made it easier for us to carry the baton, easier for us to focus on our aspirations and to have a voice
- Take a break from your work, area, surroundings which also gives your immune, nervous and digestive system a break to heal any underlying physical symptoms which may appear because of what you may be going through
- Remember to eat, sleep, breathe and exercise well to help you stay strong in mind, body, soul and spirit.

There is so much more which could be said here, however if it is of interest, continue your own research online.

Business

According to the Office of National Statistics, around 80% of businesses fail in the first year. Five years later and only around 43% of businesses are still going. These are harsh statistics to bear in mind, so no wonder people hesitate so much before going ahead, even if it is a side business i.e., not yet your main source of income.

Some people may just dive in; like their characters, they may be extroverts and high-risk takers, full of energy and passion to push ahead. However, others who may be more introvert and conscientious may hesitate and like to have all their ducks in a row before starting.

The good news is that it is not overly important what type of person you are as anyone can start a business. The not so bad news is that everyone will need to build life muscles in order to continue a business! What life muscles you may ask? Don't you just need business skills such as knowing how to do finance, marketing, sales and customer service? Well, yes, however you can beg, borrow or buy those skills in, if you don't have them all yourself. What you cannot buy are the following business life muscles:

- Tenaciousness
- Determination
- Persistency and consistency
- Passion, drive and energy

- Discipline
- Courage
- Resourcefulness
- Ability to make quick, informed decisions.

You will need all of these and more in order to be in the 57% of businesses still around in five years' time.

Just start the damn 'ting'!

Okay, so you have a great idea, have researched it and are ready to go. Then just start it! Unless you need to raise finance in the very beginning, like some tech firms, go ahead and test the market, see if people want what you are selling. The point is, you just won't know until you try. No matter what age you are, it is never too late to start a business. It could be from dog walking, to an app, to creating products to sell, to being an agent for goods to come into the country, to widgets!

Stop watching business programs and webinars and start from where you are, in your local neighbourhood, your work community, using your contacts and your knowledge. What you don't know, go and find out, as there are plenty of resources out there such as the Business Library https://www.bl.uk/business-and-ip-centre and Start Ups https://startups.co.uk/ . Even better, talk to or work with someone in the same field who has already done something similar and let them know you are learning the trade. Or partner with someone with different skills, similar products or the money. However, always make it clear in a written agreement, who is bringing what and who is doing what, as lines can become blurred. This process may take some time but it can save time and money later on.

You can learn all you want in a webinar but until you are fighting for your business to survive after spending your own money, to make money, then you haven't really committed. Of course, start it small alongside your day job and keep it there if you like, but if you want it to be your be all and end all, at some stage you will need to just jump in and 'start the damn ting!'

INSIGHT

Taking that leap of faith – Karen

When we first started out in the basement of a gym in 2009, we knew we had to at least cover the rent and reception each month. We negotiated to have the full three rooms and reception area downstairs. This was after already starting our online MindBody Therapy business with a group of likeminded therapists who would refer clients to each other. Devon was already practising as a full time therapist in various locations and I was working four days a week in corporate, having already completed a Coaching Diploma. When it came to putting down the deposit, we were the only ones in the group who, in the end, would commit, even though the lead had come from someone else in the group. We had to put the money where our mouth was and take a leap of faith. Then we had to find the therapists as well as a receptionist who would cover the times when we were not there. A trial by fire but at the time of writing this book, the business is still going!

* * * * * *

Teachment©

To succeed in business, you will need to go where others cannot or will not go. It can be a lonely road, so be prepared to boost and motivate yourself to keep going in those dark moments, but also find a way to let your hair down every so often, to release the pent-up emotions (and there will be many). You will have to dig deep and become a master muscle builder!

In the beginning

You learn quickly in business when you are just starting out that decisions have to be made pretty quickly every single day. Whether that is what sofa to buy, what to put on the windows, to what to put in the petty cash tin (yes, those days of cash!!), it's all go and people everywhere are demanding something from you. This is especially true if you have a bricks and mortar business. You learn quickly that rent, rates and employees still have to get paid whether you earned enough that week or not. You find ways to partner with people, do the right deals and get the right people in pretty quickly in order to survive.

It can be exhausting as you start to push a business up the hill to gain momentum, before it is able to roll itself.

How do you keep sane? How do you stop yourself from running away? Especially when you are working 24/7 on it.

It helps to have a partner, whether that is in the business, a life partner, a sister, friend or parent. You need someone to bounce off, someone who doesn't easily get fed up of hearing you talk about the business yet again, like it's the only thing in your life, as it literally has to be the only thing in your life during those times.

However, it also comes with immense joy and the feeling of accomplishment that you've actually started and are running your own business! You are the master of your own ship, able to work when you want, even though you end up working a lot more than you like to realise or acknowledge, especially at the beginning.

Celebrate those times whenever you can.

Along with the excitement and joy of running your own business, comes the exhaustion one to three years later, when you think you've got somewhere and then a contract collapses which wipes out part of your revenue, and you feel like you have to start all over again. Or of course a global pandemic hits everyone and it takes us into 'unprecedented' and uncertain times.

This is where determination and persistency kicks in. It is never ending and you need stamina and the courage to keep going, even when it seems hopeless. Plus, if you have staff, you will have to keep them paid and motivated at the same time, sometimes without paying yourself, which sucks!

INSIGHT

The early days – Karen

We committed to the new centre contract for a year and then set about finding therapists who would hire the spaces from us. We opened on 1st July 2009. Little did we know that at the same time another company was starting who read Devon's profile about his work in the community, and wanted to partner with us. We had to find therapists not just for the centre but also across London and the South East. Devon was still working across various places but started seeing clients Mondays, Wednesdays, Saturdays and some Sundays and I started working three days at the centre, while holding down my four day corporate job.

It was 24/7, seven days a week, fun and excitement as the gym was also starting out with great members, though we always saw them as a bonus and advertised outside the gym. Plus, we had a great set of people who came along to work with us. We had great Christmas meals as a bigger team and loads of laughter. It was exhausting but exhilarating.

* * * * * *

Teachment©

Working with people, you will have to up your game with communication and work collaboratively with them to achieve a 'win win' situation. You cannot do it all by yourself. You can stay in control but you will need to get along with people, whether they are your clients, suppliers, partners or landlord. You will have to learn to be empathetic to your staff, keep them motivated and treat them well, so you get the most out of them. You may have to clean the toilet and pay off the bank loan but keep your intent and determination for it to be worthwhile, and it will be. At least you will have many more stories to tell the grandkids!

Growth times

After a while in business, you need to decide if you are going to expand or stay as niche or small as you are. Sometimes the expansion can be what we call 'sideways growth', where you take on more people to cover the growth that is already happening, so you can meet the demands. The other expansion can be 'tall growth', where you push to find more partnerships, contracts and people with varying skills to help push the growth of the company forward.

It is here where more skills such as being a leader, being reliable, having the ability to take risks and collaborate with partners comes into play. You are no longer alone, you may have so many more people relying on you such as staff or contractors to pay, suppliers to keep happy, customers demanding your time, as well as family and friends (who are they again!), reminding you that they still need to see you and have a bit of your energy in their lives.

INSIGHT

From small boat to cruise ship – Karen

When we were three years in, we were considering moving the business, as we knew we wanted to have our own space, so people didn't have to walk through the gym before coming into our serene space. We wanted people to feel the aura, the essence, to smell the scents and breathe into a Healing Hug when they came into the centre. We could have rented two rooms for the next therapy centre, with the most successful therapists, whilst making our earnings and I could run it from home. That would have made financial sense to me, with no premises to look after and less risk taken.

However, Devon had other ideas and when a bigger centre came along instead, like a big cruise ship that could carry more people, we both said YES. This was said with faith, as we didn't have all the money it would need to transform the space from an old antique shop with few rooms, damp, no central heating and old electrics, into a warm and cosy complementary centre.

Instead of using a small boat to take us and a few people ahead in life, we now needed new skills to captain and run a cruise ship so we could, as we called it, 'for each one, touch one' even more people. I still hugged one person at a time but there were hundreds more people than before, and hopefully each one went on to hug their village. We've done all we have together, but also with a team of people who at the time we called 'family' who believed in our vision and cared enough to give excellent service to our clients.

We had to find more money. We had to find a new booking system and card payments system (we were still on cash only like most salons/centres at the time!). We had to find more equipment, more people to join us and kit out the whole place, while keeping our current business going. We had to survive, then 'do more, be more', expand our knowledge, utilise our skills, do the hard work and be persistent enough to follow our purpose and our passion.

Then we needed to thrive to success… at our level, which may be totally lower or higher than someone else's level, but that too was okay because either way, there was an underlying purpose to our mission and we felt aligned and right on time.

* * * * * *

Saying goodbye to old ways, habits, equipment or people

It is very easy to keep hold of bits of office equipment, machinery or 'we've always done it this way' types of thinking, when growth inside a business takes place. However, there comes a point when the fallback position is no longer useful or working. It is then time to admit it, say goodbye and reset. Not lightly of course, especially when there are other people involved; however we had to lose the 'family' mode and change into a business mode, always adapting with people, processes and systems.

When growing a business, there are people who start out with you who do not stay, for varying reasons, which makes it hard to say goodbye. However, it can be harder to have to let someone go, who is no longer on the same page as you and your business. You have to put your big pants on and take leadership in those moments, doing what is best for the business ahead.

Sometimes the goodbye is not physical but mentally shifting where your mind is at, to make it better for yourself, your family and how you manage your life and your business. Nothing stays the same and being adaptable is a strong life muscle we must all nurture and respect.

INSIGHT

Navigating the storms – Karen

Having to decide which bill to pay was a very current thought during the Covid pandemic, when bills were backing up, the council grants being 'given' away were not so forthcoming and the tax man still wanted his piece of the pie. It all added to the stress of running a business (albeit one with nil revenue at the time), along with a strong sense of resilience and belief that 'it's all going to be okay, there is a solution to everything' type of thinking.

However, it didn't feel like that at the time, when business owners including ourselves still had to find money to pay the excess tax on staff costs, along with empty premises. We had to adapt, pivot and look at other ways to diversify the business. It took guts, willpower, courage and personal money, as if we were just starting out again. We had to review everything and take risks with borrowing again in order to invest into the business, for whatever the next season would bring. It was like charting the seas, not knowing where land was but trusting you will reach land and that there will be enough food and water for everyone.

* * * * * *

Teachment©

Don't rush the process. There are seasons when growth is organic, natural and the hard work is paying off, and other seasons when we have to start the daily grind again, kick start a new project or bring in and train new team members. Take it all in your stride and go with the flow, as nothing stays the same and it never ALL always goes to plan.

In business with your partner

Being in business with your intimate partner is not easy, full stop. Fighting is inevitable, but learning to get over it quickly is a skill worth learning, as every day there are issues to talk about and decisions to make.

It is paramount that trust and respect are at the core of this new 'baby', as when business is not booming it is very easy to blame the other person for a 'wrong' decision made. It is essential to keep in perspective that everyone makes mistakes, but how we learn from it and bounce back is crucial.

The life muscles and tools needed are:

- Knowing each other's strengths and highlighting them
- Being willing to observe and step in to compensate for any weaknesses: to learn a new skill fast or delegate it
- Sticking up for each other and showing up when needed rather than allowing it to all fall on one person's shoulders
- Taking time with each other: patience and kindness is key
- Staying in your lane of skills and knowledge
- Regulating judgement and ego
- Recognising each other's wins
- Respecting each other's space
- Bringing humour into the middle of it all
- Looking after the 'baby' and 'US'
- Leaving the 'CEO' at the business when the key goes in the home door.

It is teamwork instead of competition, although it may be very easy to allow the ego to rage as each person has valid ideas and contributions. When each partner is a powerhouse in their own right it can be hard to back down, but just as we respect the 'US' in a relationship, it is important to respect this new 'baby'. After all, we want it to take baby steps, to become a teenager, to spread its wings; and the realisation that it is bigger than the both of us allows us to loosen the grip of, 'It's mine, it must go my way'. It is like having a right leg and a left leg; it is very difficult to reach a destination if both are trying to walk in different directions.

It may mean doing things we don't like and of course working the hours we didn't expect, but at the end of the day, it is a team and the team needs the win.

INSIGHT

Working out how to work together – Karen

In the beginning we had to get used to each other's working pattern and style. Reading the book the E-Myth revisited https://www.amazon.co.uk/Myth-Revisited-Small-Businesses-About-ebook/dp/B000RO9VJK was a lifesaver for me as I realised how different we were, hence why we were clashing! There were parts of me that were manager and doer, and parts of him that were entrepreneur and manager. He would come up with ideas and I would implement them. I would get on with all the ordering, organisation, admin and accounts and he would look after the therapy and therapists side. If we stayed in our lanes in defined roles it worked, most of the time!

We created a decision tree for different areas of the business so we could determine who had the last say if we disagreed on a matter. If it ended up in one of our expert areas where we had the knowledge and the skill, that person had the last word. It worked for us during the busy growth times so that decisions didn't linger in limbo, stalling the business.

It takes courage and sacrifice as life becomes all about the business in the early days and times of growth. It encroaches on daily life and it is important to carve out time for the 'US' as intimate partners. However, it is also exciting, exhilarating and bonding during periods of blood, sweat, tears, laughter and exhaustion.

It can tear people and businesses apart but it can also bring people and the wider community together, as family businesses create jobs up and down the country and are a backbone of our communities.

* * * * * *

Money

Going through major events such as a divorce, losing a job or business, or losing a loved one (as well as a global pandemic), can totally change how we view money and blow up our personal circumstances.

In life there are always ups and downs when it comes to money, but with no more 'jobs for life' along with the continuation of the gig economy, it can mean we experience more shock waves and changes throughout our adult life.

How do we navigate our way through it all?

INSIGHT

Childhood saving – Karen

We were taught growing up to 'spend some, save some and give some', however my Mum and Dad put a heavy emphasis on saving and made sure us girls started a Post Office savings account from primary school age. Even when we were grown, Dad always asked, 'are you saving?' The idea being to save for a rainy day: a day or days when we may need emergency funds we can turn to.

* * * * * *

Money experts often recommend saving three to six months' worth of expenses, but with the changes over the years, it is more like nine to twelve months' worth of monthly outgoings that we need to try to build up in a separate bank account.

How on earth do we pay the monthly bills at the same time or how do we save for a deposit for a house at the same time, I hear some say?

INSIGHT

Finding a way – Karen

When our parents came to England from Jamaica, they could not afford to live in a whole house or flat. They usually had to share rooms with other people, often in appalling conditions following signs of 'no blacks, no dogs, no Irish'. They came with experiences of owning shops, nursing, farming, carpentry and other trades, only to find themselves having to take factory or cleaning jobs due to their 'lower class' status: nignogs, coons, blackies and the n-word.

I don't know how they managed amidst blatant racism, but their resilience meant that they pulled together to save using what they called a 'pardner system', where the community put in regular weekly monies and one person takes out a set large amount at a time, so that one by one, they could save and build enough deposit for a house. Basically, they were paying by instalments built on trust rather than a bank loan, for which black people at the time were largely turned down anyway. Even then, they had to rent each room and still live in one room in order to afford to pay the mortgage, until room-by-room, they claimed back their house (as they had children or saved more money or got a better job).

We didn't have much but we had love and discipline. We knew not to even bother to ask for certain things like the latest trainers, as the white plimsolls would always do, be it from the market or C&A. We were left wearing odd coloured coats and clothes, whatever was affordable in the sales, and could not complain about our hand me downs.

We were grateful for food on the table, albeit sometimes soup with not much meat in (except in Dad's, so we would sit by his side while he ate so he might put a little for us on his side plate… happy days!). Eventually, our parents saved enough for a caravan holiday, booked via Daltons weekly newspaper, the cheapest they could find. We were just glad to have a 'real' holiday!

* * * * * *

If our 'Windrush' parents could find a way, surely we, with all our mod cons and access to so much knowledge and privilege, can find a way?

Yes it was a different banking system then, however, as leftovers from colonial Britain, they still went through crisis, racism, job loss, rejection, high mortgage rates, housing crashes, four children and major changes in their lives; but they were determined to live a certain way, so they found a way.

What are you willing to do to live the life you hope for?

Are you willing to do things such as:

- ☐ Take on a lodger
- ☐ Ask the bank of Mum and Dad
- ☐ Take on that extra job
- ☐ Work extra hours
- ☐ Sell something
- ☐ Downsize
- ☐ Set saving goals and automate them, so that as soon as you get paid, a standing order will save a portion in a different bank account
- ☐ Pay off bad debt – there is plenty of help online
- ☐ Save on bills by using bill switching sites
- ☐ Using money advice sites to do a budget and stick to it to reduce debt and increase savings
- ☐ Up skill for better opportunities
- ☐ Stop...Breathe...Think.

Could we also get used to living with less?

INSIGHT

Make do and mend – Karen

'Stuff, stuff, stuff' as my Dad would always say! He would put tape around a broomstick before even thinking of buying a new one and newspaper in his slippers and his shoes, using the good old Blakey's (metal piece) to correct the instep from wear and tear on the sole of his shoe. We can all learn a lesson from him on 'saving the pennies, so the pounds look after themselves'.

Keep it simple – Devon

Give me sardines, flour and water and I can make dumplings and sardines for my dinner, or I used to buy a whole chicken or meat and save the oil for frying an egg. Hardly anything was thrown away when I was forced to live by myself, sharing a room. Nowadays it would seem like hard times to some people when they cannot afford a take away! Their focus is on that, rather than on seeing how much money they could save by buying simple products.

* * * * * *

Reasons for us to build better life muscles with money:

- Being able to save to buy that special purchase
- Greater freedom: whether we earn £100,000 or £10,000 we could end up with the same amount left, depending on what we spend. It's all relative
- Ability to give our children not just stuff but a 'leg

up' in life, whether that is paid healthcare, a car, a savings account, help with education or money towards living or a house

- Lower stress levels if we feel more in control
- Saving when young means money accumulates and compounds, especially in pension pots or stocks and shares ISA – which usually gives us more choices later in life
- We will always have an emergency fund or access to borrow some
- We will sleep better
- We will 'see' where our hard earned money is going.

Teachment©

If you feel like getting a takeaway, you could challenge yourself to also save the same amount in a separate bank account or jar, so that at the end of a month, you will be able to see how much you could save by not having it, or having it less. By all means have the takeaway, but know how much it costs and what it is doing to your savings / budget.

- Make a plan with some milestones and stick with it. Feel the joy of reaching the first milestone and push on. You will have to make some sacrifices, so decide what your priorities will be and keep in mind the bigger picture.
- Live within your means, don't spend more than you have coming in.
- Develop a wise money mindset. Some rich people stay rich because they don't use their own money

but get good debt: they use other people's money to create generational wealth over the years.

- Fast money can be destructive. If sweat goes into bringing in money then we value it more, but if someone gives it to us or we inherit it, that life muscle has not been worked as hard. There is no memory of the winter months, digging the soil and in springtime planting those seeds.
- Study how others do it to discover more available choices.

PART FOUR

Trust that the Universe has your Back

Trust that you are not alone. You come from a long line of ancestors who wish the best for you. You can tap into One Energy and draw upon Nature's power, where seeds take time to grow. You can relinquish the controls when there is no need for you to micro manage, and allow yourself to walk in the flow where life aligns and brings you what you need. It is all happening perfectly, despite any chaos.

Chapter 9
Seasons of Life

Learning to trust in life is a daily balancing practice of knowing what we know, yet accepting we know nothing. Of being open, aware and 'listening', yet laser focused on where we are going and what we are doing. Of understanding, learning and growing amidst the obstacles and pain, yet choosing and trusting in life that 'all is well'.

There are times when we need to plan and strive forward in life, examining ourselves and growing where we need to, yet other times when we need to allow the growth to prove itself, like bread, and embed into our lives by standing still. By being still you can also leap forward at the same time. This is the paradox of life.

At these times, we need to trust the Universe and allow the stillness, even if we are screaming inside our heads, 'when is it going to happen for me?! Why am I still waiting!'

Stop. Breathe. Reset.

Like the natural seasons, we cannot hurry a blossom or make a fruit grow. Of course we can plan, take action, ask, believe and receive but let go of being attached to how it all unveils.

How hard it is for us sometimes to allow life to unfold, to be patient enough to allow ourselves, and occasionally those around us, to grow and blossom. We soon realise that we cannot force something or someone to be ready, just because we think we are. Before we know it, a little 'nasty' area of our life gets thrown up or we get challenged, and we soon realise we still have some learning to do. In fact, we all know that we are never really done; as long as we have breath, we can become an even better 'spirit of love' in this human body and do better, be better.

Teachment©

Yes, do the work but don't rush the seasons; sit down and enjoy each one. They are forever changing, as nothing stays the same for long. Accept where you are in life, the age you are, the job you have, the love you have, the people you have in your life, for that is your season and you cannot forge ahead without experiencing it and appreciating it on some level.

Spring

Spring is a time of getting the soil ready and for planting seeds, all in the excitement of an expected harvest in autumn. Some seeds are already starting to come through without us doing anything, such as bluebells and daffodils, which flower every year. Blossoms start appearing and life looks good as we start to see something happening.

Spring can remind us to renew, refresh and revitalise areas in our lives. Like building life muscles, some seeds are already planted; we've already done the work, we've already worked on ourselves and are starting to see small movements, such as a breakthrough in our relationships, career advancement or more satisfaction and joy in our daily life. It can also draw more light on areas which we need to look at, as the increasing light highlights any cobwebs or dust we may need to clear out of our lives, such as habits or people, which can be a necessary challenge that life is putting in front of us.

The Age of Spring – Identity

The Spring of life's season is a time when we are in our late teens/ 20s to 30s when we have the get up and go, the energy to explore and plunge into the unknown, to take risks, to scale mountains literally and to start the process of looking after ourselves. This is when adult things can seem so boring and unnecessary, like realising how to handle money, sex, food, drink, pay the rent and work stuff all at the same time.

Amongst the fun, it is an important time for us to put on big adult pants and for our parents to allow us to take responsibility, to fall and get ourselves back up on our feet. This is where we should be able to handle bigger stuff than in our teens, such as work, contributing to the household, giving back and sowing the right seeds for our future life. It is a time when we start deciding for ourselves what parts of our upbringing we want to take forward and which parts we want to discard, to prepare our own life path for ourselves and others who we choose to be in our life.

We may still be a bit unsure of ourselves as we are trying to find our identity. However, we are sure that we want to be independent and free from parental pressures and expectations. It is a time of hunting not only for our soul mate, but for all things in life to see what matches us, our lifestyle, our spirit.

We need to build life muscles such as:

- Building confidence in ourselves and our choices, rather than being persuaded by what others think we should want
- Focusing on the facts not the dramatics, especially from external factors
- Having the ability to set goals and see them through
- Being able to take on responsibility plus any consequences of our actions
- Increasing our ability to cope, knowing that we have some of the controls in our hands
- Seeing each challenge not as a threat but an opportunity
- Being assured rather than unsettled, even when we are not sure which way to go
- Knowing that it is okay to not be okay, and calling for help when we need it
- Drawing on inner strength to find the will to keep putting one foot in front of the other.

Summer

Summer is a beautiful time when flowers are blossoming. Everything always looks better as fruit starts to appear and it feels wonderful, warm and sunny. It is a time to sit back and feel like all our hard work has paid off. It is not quite time to reap but it looks really promising. Summer is also a time to have fun, play and enjoy the nature pouring out of the ground. However, we still have to remember to stay on track and not allow the heat to ruin the growth; so watering more often, to bring the balance and allow the growth spurts to take place. Also, being mindful of plucking out the weeds which grow extremely fast at this time.

As in life, we realise that it was worth hanging around in winter, hibernating, working on our craft and being still. It was worth looking at the dry twigs and pruning them, to get more fruit. It was worth all that time sowing the seeds, as we marvel at the growth that may be happening in our life.

We feel we have arrived, we feel excited when it all seems to be finally going our way, and we feel joy, love and generosity towards all those around us.

The Age of Summer – Growth

This Summer of life's season is when we are in our late 20s/ 30s to 40s. We are thriving in our chosen career, job, pursuit of passion (or we feel we should be), and growth spurts are common. We naturally (especially many women due to our womb) feel like we are ready for nesting within a family, while still rising in our positions in life. We feel we are in the prime of our life; no longer the awkward teenager who thought they knew everything, yet knew nothing. Now we really know our stuff and we usually have some money to prove it.

We feel that the world is our oyster and that we could conquer it all if we wanted to. We are brave and brazen in the work place and not afraid to say what's on our mind. We push for what seems right, while reinforcing our own truth of what we stand for, what our rights are and who we feel we should have in our lives. The rewards are vast and varied and we are in the prime of our lives, as we plan projects both in work and outside work and create bonds with our soul mate, friends and colleagues.

We are strengthening life muscles such as:

- Staying positive and focused amidst changing goal posts and landscapes
- Controlling anxiety and worry by drawing on our experiences, knowing we have the inner strength to keep us going
- Being able to visualise ahead for ourselves and our family
- Building endurance levels of the body and mind through repetitive exercise and reading
- Recovering quickly when we receive emotional wounds from words or situations
- Staying balanced while trying to juggle family and work responsibilities
- Recovering quickly from setbacks and always looking for solutions
- Building mental stamina to study, gain knowledge and/or experience to jump ahead in our career and chosen lifestyle.

Autumn

Time to reap! Time to pick the fruit off the tree. Sometimes we have an abundance of produce that we need to give away otherwise it may spoil, and other times the harvest we expected doesn't come and instead of bountiful fruit, we are left with just enough for one person. It could be our fault, if we didn't prune when we should have, or maybe we didn't water enough, prepare for blight or remove the bugs. Or it could just be that there was not enough sun this year.

We need to build enough life muscles to take us through these lean seasons, as we may not always get what we think we should, at the time we think we should. Despite all our hard work and dedication, we just didn't get that job, our child never got into that school, our relationship goes stale or the business was in the wrong place at the wrong time.

We have to learn to say 'Thank You' and move on, which is easier said than done. It may just be a mental moving on inside of you, to find better ways to revive a relationship, to build understanding between you and your child or understand your position within an organisation. It is time to let go of what was, understand why there was no growth and learn from any mistakes.

If it WAS a great harvest, you could be basking in the array of fruit and enjoying the rewards of your hard work in life: 'the cat who got the cream'. Maybe you got the job or the promotion, maybe you went on holiday and renewed your wedding vows, or your children passed their exams and got into that university. Then it is a time to enjoy and celebrate all that hard work and say 'Thank You' for the harvest.

The Age of Autumn – Influence

The Autumn of life's season is towards our late 40s into our 50s and early 60s. A time when we are fully reaping from all our hard work and dedication to our craft, our job, our hobby, our children, our spiritual life, our business. Or it could be a time of change, where the kids have grown up and we realise we have nothing in common with our partner, or we become disillusioned by life and work and decide to go it alone.

If we are reaping and enjoying the harvest of our life, celebrate this beautiful time. We deserve it. We've put the work in, we've been patient, we've said our piece already in the work place; we know we can either stay there or leave. We have the skills, character and knowledge others will headhunt us for. We have influence and we have power. We feel comfortable with who we are, no one can push us over unless we allow them to, as we have been wearing big adult pants for years.

Even if we are feeling 'burnt out' or if we are starting out again, there must be areas of our life that feel good, that feel right, where we feel supported. It could feel tumultuous but by now, we have learned and can accept that this too is a season and it hurts but it will not last. Previous experience has told us so, our life muscles confirm that. We may find ourselves mulling over our own lives rather than running to friends to chat through like we did in our 30s, as we realise, 'we got this', it's just going to take a while.

Sometimes, we feel we have not learned anything at all and we are right back to square one. It is then when we need to draw upon our knowledge and realise that every:

- Breakdown can be a Breakthrough
- Rejection can lead to Rejuvenation
- Setback can be a Set Up for a comeback
- Obstacle can be an Opportunity.

We need to then muster our energy to go with the flow of this season and gather strength to start moving forward again, with a plan to position ourselves where we want to be and who with, along with how we want to BE at this stage of our lives.

Women at this stage in life

In our 50s/60s as women, if it hasn't already started, we will experience the menopause, which signifies the end of our menstrual cycle. As discussed previously, we are no longer a girl, or a teenager having our first period, or a woman in full bloom ready for nesting, or feeling like a powerful confident woman in full flow. However we are still viable, we just need to find our feet again.

It can also happen to be a time when any brood we have may be 'flying the nest' or at least living life without our input. They need us, they don't need us, they need us, they don't need us, it's this weird push and pull, yet we know they are leaving us and we have to let them go. We cannot clip their wings, no matter how useless it may make us feel, that our 'mothering' days are over. It may be yet another grieving that we have to go through during this season.

* * * * * *

Be mindful at this time to build life muscles such as:

- Being less discouraged over setbacks, knowing that you have the strength to pull through or change direction
- Looking for solutions to become more accomplished, when we feel like we haven't achieved enough
- Being proactive in looking for solutions/coping strategies to the hormonal changes in our bodies
- Being more adaptable to change rather than getting stale in our ways
- Seeing the larger picture to keep it all in perspective
- The ability to bounce back from failure or rejection without useless addictions
- Being able to think more clearly, taking stress and overwhelm into peace and calm
- Seeing the beauty in it all and being grateful for all we DO have
- Bringing forth calm, hope, faith and love from our 'memory capsules'
- Bringing in forgiveness for ourselves and others, over all that has happened in our lives
- Accepting who and where we are, with kindness.

Winter

The days are getting colder and darker and the harvest is done. There may be a few winter greens hanging around, but the beauty of blossoms and fruit is long gone and it is time to cut back and sort out the land. It is a time where we do not spend as much time outdoors and tend to draw the curtains earlier to enjoy the warmth inside.

We may change our clothing as the jumpers, boots and coats come out and we prepare ourselves for winter. In this same way, we need to build our life muscles ready for rough times, so we can manage. It is a time to put on our superpower cloak of protection to ride out any storms ahead.

Winter is a time to ponder all the learning that has taken place that year. A time to consider, hibernate and restore, to buckle down the hatches and make sure we have enough wood on the fire. It is a time to sit, daydream, prepare and plan what we would like to do in the seasons to come, but also to sit and be grateful for the seasons we just had and still say 'Thank You, I enjoyed that or I endured, I survived, I thrived, I learned loads, I didn't expect it to turn out like this but I'm okay'.

The Age of Winter – Legacy

The Winter of life's season is when we are in our late 60s and 70s, when our life's work as we know it may be concluding, and/or we have to find a different way to work, maybe part time. Although some people, especially if there has been a break-up, are acutely aware that they may have to work in some form or fashion until they are 75 to pay off the new mortgage, rebuild a pension pot or pay the rent.

At the same time, we may be reviewing our lives: what we have done or not done and may still have a full bucket list to complete, wondering when on earth we are going to get all that done. Maybe medications have started to kick in and we are experiencing more aches and pains. Or maybe we have found a new lease of life and started a new exercise regime, which is keeping us active as well as keeping away certain ailments.

Either way, we see retirement looming and start looking up the state pension (UK) to see when we can dare to think of retiring fully. We may wonder at our legacy, start having regrets about work, our relationships and any family bonds that may still need healing, along with looking to move somewhere quieter, all at the same time. We may also be celebrating, looking forward to just doing whatever hobby takes our fancy and having a big party to mark retirement and a new wave of freedom.
In our 70s to 90s, post retirement, we may have grandchildren and great grandchildren around to keep us young, or maybe loneliness starts to kick in as we realise we have no one. There could be lots of great memories and albums full of pictures, or regrets about our lot in life, full of pain and medication. We start thinking about legacy; what are we leaving behind and what has it all been for? We may be leaving our family material things, but what are we leaving as far as love memories, happiness, and joy are concerned? How have we impacted people around us or is it too late?

We may realise we still have to keep going even if our partner has passed on and we have to find the meaning of life all over again, as well as some clubs or activities to keep the grey matter ticking over.

INSIGHT

Family reflections – Karen

At the time of writing, our beloved Mummy would have been around 82 years old, enjoying retirement with our Dad, five years older at 87 years old. However, she passed away suddenly in December 2006 and Dad had to accept life without the many holidays, jolly bus rides and enjoying the garden together.

After the shock, the searching and despair, he reorganised himself and found a new routine, plus he still had his foundation of faith, his spiritual life muscles. He still had church, his gardening and the allotment, hobbies that kept him active and helped him to cope. Also, importantly, he had the strength and love from his family; except that in reality, after a while, we couldn't be there with him 24/7. So we were glad that he continued to enjoy his own activities, finding peace with himself and God, accepting this path he wouldn't have chosen.

* * * * * *

Wherever we find ourselves at these times, let's be mindful to build life muscles so we can:

- Diminish fear and give us a sense of empowerment to still contribute to life
- Receive insight into the 'what and why' of our lives and the feeling of the divine to bring peace as we reflect over our lives
- Remain centred and balanced
- Tap into gratefulness, happiness, joy, feelings of love to continue to see the good in people, despite what might sometimes seem like a world of pain
- Stay within our higher self and take the higher ground in situations, especially with family
- Continue to build faith: the ability to stand strong in adversity
- Show and share with others, all the life building muscles and tools which have helped you through life
- Holding onto your confidence and maintaining your tenaciousness for life
- Keep humour and laughter
- Continue to trust that the Universe has our Back.

Whichever season of life we are in, know that it is never too late to turn it around, to learn to celebrate each season. We are all human, experiencing similar emotions and phases of life, yet we are all so different and unique, so will likely revisit different seasons throughout our lives at different times.

Let's remember to talk to each other, to share our experiences with our peers, our family and our support groups, and know that we are never as alone as we think we are.

Teachment©

We come from a long line of ancestors who wish the best for us. We can tap into One Energy and draw upon Nature's power. Walk in the flow, where life aligns and brings you what you need. Know what and who is paramount in your life. Be fully present with those people.

'It's all going to be okay… it is all happening perfectly right now, this minute. I trust that the Universe has my Back'.

Help to reach out for:

- Samaritans – Call 116 123 or email jo@samaritans.org
- Contact us - Citizens Advice - https://www.citizensadvice.org.uk/
- Domestic Violence / Abuse helpline - Home | Refuge National Domestic Abuse Helpline (nationaldahelpline.org.uk) Call 0808 2000 247
- Valerie's Law | Sistah Space Sistahspace.org
- BACP - British Association for Counselling and Psychotherapy (bacp.co.uk)
- https://nationaldebtadviceline.org.uk/
- Racism and mental health | How To Deal With Racism | YoungMinds
- Read up on issues which may be affecting you - HelpGuide.org
- Age UK - https://www.ageuk.org.uk/
- About us | Independent Age
- Mind https://www.mind.org.uk/
- NHS https://www.nhs.uk/

Recommended self-help reading

Area of Life	Book	Author
Life goals	Power Up For The Year	Karen Burke
Myself, family, community	The Calming Book Of Healing Hugs	Devon & Karen Burke
Forgiveness	Forgiveness	Iyanla Vanzant
In business with partners or family / building a team	E-Myth Revisited	Michael E Gerber
Starting a business	Anyone Can Do It	Sahir & Bobby Hashemi
Money	Think And Grow Rich	Napolean Hill
Work	Shift Your Brilliance	Simon T Bailey
Menopause	Confessions Of A Menopausal Woman	Andrea McLean
Daily meditation	A Year Of Miracles	Marianne Williamson
Daily meditation	Faith In The Valley	Iyanla Vanzant
Mindfulness	The Power Of Now	Eckhart Tolle
Lifestyle and Reset thinking	You Can If You Think You Can	Norman Vincent Peale
Reset thinking	The Four Agreements	Don Miguel Ruiz
Spiritual & lifestyle	The Seven Spiritual Laws Of Success	Deepak Chopra
Spiritual	Ask And It Is Given	Esther & Jerry Hicks
Spiritual	There Is A Spiritual Solution To Everything	Wayne Dyer

Spread the word on Building Life Muscles

#Lifemuscles

Book into 1-2-1's, attend workshops and read further books with Devon and Karen. Or buy our books for your team to help them discover themselves and how they can develop resilience and find solutions.

Visit our websites for upcoming events, workshops and books from Karen and Devon Burke, as well as signups for free tools, blogs and downloads.

Buy Karen's Power Up book
https://www.amazon.co.uk/Power-Up-Year-Can-Do-ebook/dp/B08XQQTK6N

Buy their book, the Calming book of Healing Hugs
https://amzn.to/31dsrnW

Work with Karen or Devon via 1-2-1 online treatments https://bit.ly/2L3R6mG or via workshops for your teams. Corporate Bookings – MindBody Therapy (therapy4life.net)

MindBody products are available to buy online such as sprays; smudge sticks, charcoal, resin plus Devon's powerful Carib and Calm range. Also check out our latest Healing Hugs room mists. http://phore.st/r3Gyf

Join in with our monthly One Energy Systems of Healing Reiki sessions where people discuss spirituality, life and also experience group reiki share. Events – MindBody Therapy (therapy4life.net)

MindBody Publishing: www.MindBodyPublishing.net
MindBody Therapy Group Business: www.therapy4life.net

Social Enterprise: www.T4H.org.uk
Instagram: MBTherapy | Twitter: @mindbodytalk
Facebook & LinkedIn: MindBodyTherapyCentre
Linktree: https://linktr.ee/Karen_F_Burke

Manifestation

Win / win consciousness when we started the centre 'We aim to centre ourselves within the uncertainty of the gap, where our intentions and desires are planted then released in the fertile ground of pure potentiality, where we expect them to bloom when the season is right. We aim to let the Universe handle the details and trust that what is ours is being orchestrated for us, to us all. We relinquish our attachment to the outcome and choose to endeavour to enjoy every moment in this journey called life!'

Inspired by Deepak Chopra
'The Seven Spiritual Laws of Succçess'

Carpe Diem - Seize the Day

Today is the outcome of yesterday
Tomorrow, will be the outcome of Today.
You choose.

Karen Burke

ABOUT THE AUTHORS

Karen Burke, ACMA, MAAT, DipPPC

Karen is passionate about expanding people's self awareness and power, ensuring everyone she works with, has that 'Healing Hug' they need, where she is in their corner, championing them, their career and/or their businesses. She is inspiring, positive, an implementer and loves to multi-task. Her core values are integrity, honesty, loyalty and respect.

She is a business owner, Power Up Coach, Author, Speaker and Accountant, offering Accountancy and Coaching services to individuals and small businesses, looking to start, restart or power up their life and/or business.

Karen F Burke | Twitter | LinkedIn | Linktr.ee

Devon Burke

Devon believes that we are all spiritual beings on a human journey. His approach is always based in spirituality and that there is only One Energy on earth regardless of what name is attached to it. Above all, it is an individual's intent which shapes and directs their world and outcome. He is a firm believer of Karma that whatever we put out will come back to us in some shape or form, either in this life or another to come.

He has been a qualified Advanced Massage Therapist and Reiki Master for over 25 years. He is a pioneer of the Caribbean Heat Massage©, MindBody Tuning© and the One Energy Systems of Healing©. Devon uses the MindBody Therapy approach. This is a natural approach, which seeks to promote balance and well being to the whole person.

Devon Burke | LinkedIn

Printed in Great Britain
by Amazon

78026469R00129